THE ENTERTAINING COOK

THE
ENTERTAINING
COOK

PETER GLADWIN

WARD LOCK

To my three small sons who provided a constant distraction from writing this book

Food photography by Mike Evans
Food for photography prepared by
Peter Gladwin and Olivia Stewart Cox

Text set in Baskerville by Litho Link Ltd.,
Welshpool, Powys, Wales
Printed in Great Britain by The Bath Press, Avon

British Library Cataloguing in Publication Data
Gladwin, Peter
    The entertaining cook.
    1. Cookery
    I. Title
    641.568

    ISBN 0-7063-7009-0

Contents

CONTENTS

CONTENTS

Useful Weights and Measures

NOTES FOR AMERICAN READERS

In America dry goods and liquids are conventionally measured by the standard 8-oz cup. When translating pints, and fractions of pints, Americans should bear in mind that the U.S. pint is equal to 16 fl oz or 2 cups, whereas the Imperial pint is equal to 20 fl oz.

EQUIVALENT METRIC/ AMERICAN MEASURES

LIQUID MEASURES

METRIC/ IMPERIAL	AMERICAN
150 ml/¼ pint	⅔ cup
300 ml/½ pint	1¼ cups
450 ml/¾ pint	2 cups
600 ml/1 pint	2½ cups
900 ml/1½ pints	3¾ cups
1 litre/1¾ pints	4 cups (2 U.S. pints)

WEIGHTS

450 g/1 lb butter or margarine	2 cups (4 sticks)
100 g/4 oz grated cheese	1 cup
450 g/1 lb flour	4 cups
450 g/1 lb granulated sugar	2 cups
450 g/1 lb icing sugar	3½ cups confectioners' sugar
200 g/7 oz raw long-grain rice	1 cup
100 g/4 oz cooked long-grain rice	1 cup
100 g/4 oz fresh white breadcrumbs	2 cups

OVEN TEMPERATURES

Whenever the oven is used, the required setting is given as three alternatives: degrees Celsius (°C), degrees Fahrenheit (°F) and gas.

The temperature settings given are for conventional ovens. If you have a fan oven, adjust the temperature according to the manufacturer's instructions.

°C	°F	GAS
110	225	¼
120	250	½
140	275	1
150	300	2
160	325	3
180	350	4
190	375	5
200	400	6
220	425	7
230	450	8
240	475	9

INTRODUCTION

If I have a reputation, it would be on the one hand as a professional chef cooking for grand occasions and on the other as a self-confessed cheat. This book is a collection of my favourite deceptions, short-cuts and ideas. It ranges from genuine cookery advice to blatant cheating to help your entertaining. The sole aim is to produce stunning food with the minimum of time and effort and the simplest of ingredients.

There are five main recipe chapters, dealing with different types of occasion. I have also included light-hearted guidelines on how to be a successful cheat.

My intention is to persuade you that culinary cheating is in itself an art. I hope you enjoy the book and I wish you happy entertaining.

Peter Gladwin

The Rules
of an
Entertaining
Cheat

You may have thought that the very nature of cheating meant that rules would not apply, but on the contrary the rules under which I am prepared to encourage you to cheat are all very important – not least so that you are not found out!

GOOD COOKING

First and foremost it is essential you continue your efforts to cook well. I believe most of us who entertain at home do at least try to cook reasonably well and I can only repeat what many cookery writers have said before: understand your recipe before you start, taste frequently and season with thought.

FRESH AND SIMPLE INGREDIENTS

Ingredients do not have to be exotic or extraordinary to achieve original and exciting dishes. The good cheat uses unusual combinations of the most simple fresh ingredients to achieve wonderful results.

PRESENT YOUR FOOD NATURALLY BUT BEAUTIFULLY

Presentation is everything and it is all too easy to spoil the effect of a dish by rushing the final stages. Take care your garnishes are in place, make sure your sauces don't dribble. Add colour and contrast wherever you can. Even a hard-boiled egg can look stunning if you add a watercress sprig and an edible nasturtium alongside it.

DON'T APOLOGIZE

The English seem to have a national habit of receiving a compliment with a denial – 'It was easy' or 'I am sorry it was not meant to turn out like that'. If a dish you have prepared is praised, accept the compliment with grace and don't be tempted to apologize instead.

DON'T GIVE AWAY SECRETS

All too often when you are pleased with a new recipe you eagerly give it to others. A month later you bitterly regret the indiscretion when the dish is served on someone else's table. The good cheat must never explain or share his or her secrets.

CHEAT WITH SUBTLETY AND FINESSE

This book is not about smothering chicken in some overpowering glutinous sauce and then pretending it is duck; nor saving a fine claret bottle and decanting 'plonk' into it. Unfortunately it cannot be guaranteed that your guests will be totally devoid of palate. Cheating well involves subtlety and finesse: the best use of prepared fresh food from a supermarket or delicatessen, the substitute of one ingredient for a much simpler one and the careful accumulation and use of tips or short-cuts.

KITCHEN MAGIC

The kitchen is a very revealing room. For many of us it is the room in which we spend most time and a lot can be learnt from its tidiness, homeliness or sophistication. I don't recommend innumerable 'time-saving' gadgets (although since the day I was unwillingly persuaded to buy a dishwasher, I have never looked back) but the successful cheat uses his or her kitchen to great advantage and takes trouble to create an atmosphere of good cooking.

A string of onions, a spice shelf, fresh herbs hanging upside-down to dry, volumes of Mrs Beeton and an assortment of wooden chopping blocks and utensils – these are the trappings of the good cook. If you want to go a step further, fry a crushed clove of garlic just before your guests arrive – I guarantee you will get at least one 'something smells exceedingly good'.

Perhaps you would like a little more practical advice on what a good cheat uses in the kitchen.

THE FOOD PROCESSOR

It is most important to understand the limitations of a food processor: it does not chop, it purées; it does not mix, it blends; and it does not slice to any self-respecting standard. That said, it can be an invaluable aid to making soups, sauces, puddings and many other dishes.

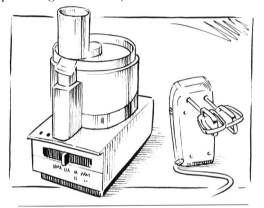

ELECTRIC HAND WHISK

More necessary than a food processor is a small electric hand whisk. They are not expensive and can save you both time and effort without any loss of quality. Anything that your grandmother's recipe book told you to beat by hand can be achieved with an electric hand whisk. It gives you complete control and is ideal for meringues, soufflés, mayonnaise and so on.

MICROWAVE OVEN

I have yet to master the art of microwave cooking and I have therefore not included any such recipes in this book. I would not, however, wish to discourage its use as a cheat's device if you have one. Just remember my first principles: do not tell and do not apologize. At home we successfully use a microwave oven for reheating vegetables and sauces or defrosting that vital forgotten ingredient.

KNIVES AND ELECTRIC CARVING KNIVES

Alas, there is no cheat's substitute for a good sharp knife – resorting to an electric carving knife is merely an acceptance that your other knives are blunt and I promise you that if you use a really sharp knife, you will see the difference. A good butcher will usually grind a knife for you but many kitchen knives are simply worn out. So rather than an electric carving knife, try a new all-purpose cook's knife.

WOK

Of all the authentic and basic cooking implements why a wok? Once you become familiar with using a wok it is an invaluable kitchen aid. It provides instant shallow frying, an even heat, no burning edges and very little washing up. Always rinse your wok immediately after use while it is still hot and then keep it oiled ready for action.

SPECIAL UTENSILS

In any good cook shop you will find all sorts of small, occasionally mystifying utensils, some of which can be of great help. They also make excellent inexpensive presents and I do recommend the following:

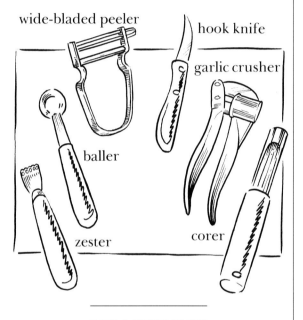

wide-bladed peeler

hook knife

garlic crusher

baller

zester

corer

MEASURING

Contrary to popular belief, professional cooks do in fact measure their ingredients and it would therefore be ill advised for cheats like us not to do so. A decent set of scales and a measuring jug are both important but measuring with spoons can be very useful to save time.

25 g/1 oz flour	= 1 rounded tbsp
25 g/1 oz caster sugar	= 1 rounded tbsp
25 g/1 oz icing sugar	= 1 heaped tbsp
25 g/1 oz grated cheese	= 2 rounded tbsp
15 g/½ oz gelatine	= 3 tsp

IN THE REFRIGERATOR

My main advice would be to leave room for specific ingredients and finished dishes that need chilling. However, there are a few things which will aid your cheating repertoire if you always keep them in stock:

natural yogurt
fromage frais
ready-grated cheese
light cream cheese
pesto sauce
tomato purée
good quality mayonnaise
carton custard
all sorts of stocks
    (cubes or cartons)
bottled lemon juice
ready-made beurre manié
        (equal quantities
        of flour and fat
        blended together
        for thickening hot
        liquids)

homemade vinaigrette
        (3 parts oil to 1
        part wine vinegar;
        Dijon mustard,
        lemon juice,
        crushed garlic,
        parsley, chives,
        salt, pepper and
        sugar – all to
        taste)

onions
lemons
fresh herbs (especially parsley)

EASY SHOPPING

Undoubtedly the easiest possible way to shop is to get someone else to do it for you, but even then it can be frustrating if items are forgotten or incorrect. Anyway, let's assume you will do it yourself. The first essential is a sensible shopping list.

THE SHOPPING LIST

A good shopping list needs to be detailed enough to avoid forgetting items but flexible enough to take advantage of the freshest and best ingredients available. Items such as butter, eggs and cooking oil are easily forgotten and need to be listed. To specify salad items or vegetables, however, is restrictive and while your list should remind you to buy these, you are better off seeing what is the best produce in the store on a particular day.

I also recommend you keep a running shopping list for special ingredients. That way when you run out of garam masala or dried ceps, you immediately put it on your running list. Don't you?

THE SHOPS

The next decision is where to shop – a choice usually determined by proximity, preference and pocket. We all know that there are some major stores brimming with high quality, high priced, ready-prepared food but who do they think they are fooling? The good cheat does not want packet food – he just wants less effort in preparing his own dishes.

Supermarkets are marvellous for personal choice, freshness and availability of special items. Their quick turnover and amazing buying power tend to ensure good quality but the range and eye appeal can sometimes distract you from what you actually wanted to buy.

The small shopkeeper has to survive on reputation and service to his customers. He will usually go out of his way to help you and this must not be under-estimated. I therefore advise you to choose the right shop for the right purpose and not to completely neglect your local suppliers.

USING YOUR SHOPKEEPERS

There is an art in making the best use of the shopkeepers themselves. The butcher or fishmonger will be delighted to show off his skills by boning, chining, gutting or scaling. Rather than mastering all these arduous tasks, the self-respecting cheat just learns how to ask nicely that they be done.

THE DELICATESSEN

Delicatessens are inspirational places. Although quite expensive they are usually filled with desirable edibles and often run by enthusiastic cooks who will be eager to spout advice on the maturity of cheese or the complementary flavours of charcuterie.

CONVENIENCE FOODS

Convenience foods have undoubtedly found their place in everyday living but have little relevance in stylish entertaining. It still amazes me that such large and mouthwatering packages can contain such miniscule and unexciting products. The best of the convenience foods appear to be the puddings and as a last resort I think you could buy them. Generally, however, simple and original use of fresh ingredients will do you more credit.

SUBSTITUTES

One of the most useful skills to acquire is knowing the right substitute. I have already mentioned that your shopping list should not be too inflexible but even so if your recipe says sorrel and sorrel is out of season, what do you buy instead? Or if your recipe says whiting, will rock salmon do? I have detailed below a rather unconventional list of suggested substitutes. I am not claiming that each one will give the same results, but in most recipes the ingredients I have suggested ought to be interchangeable.

Meat, game and poultry

Turkey, poussin	Chicken
Goose	2 Ducks
Veal	Young pork
Calves' liver or kidneys	Lamb's liver or kidneys
Lardon	Thick bacon
Specific game bird	Mainly interchangeable but cooking times will differ

Fish

Turbot	Halibut
Salmon	Sea trout
Lobster	Crayfish or monkfish
Sole	Plaice or dab
Red snapper	Grouper
Hake	Haddock
Whiting	Cod
Scampi	Prawns or monkfish

Fats

Lard	Vegetable suet (for pastry)
Margarine	Oil (for frying)
Butter	Margarine
Soured cream	Yogurt
Single cream	Fromage frais
Double cream	Crème fraîche (not whiskable)

Fruit and vegetables

Endive	Frisée
Oak leaf lettuce	Lollo rosso
Broccoli	Cauliflower
Sorrel	Spinach and lemon juice
Lime	Lemon
Aubergine	Beef tomatoes
Spring onion	White onion
Mushroom	Types interchangeable
Pears	Apples
Damsons	Plums
Peaches	Nectarines

Herbs and spices

Garlic	Shallots or onions
Chives	Spring onion
Chervil	Parsley
Basil	Pesto sauce
Tarragon	Tarragon vinegar
Oregano	Marjoram
Mint	Borage (that was helpful!)
Aniseed	Fennel
Caraway	Sesame
Saffron	Turmeric
Allspice	Mixed ground cloves, cinnamon and nutmeg
Five-spice	Cinnamon, cayenne pepper, ginger and any other spices
Cinnamon	Cloves
Mace	Nutmeg
Garam masala	Cloves, cardamom, black pepper

Miscellaneous

Brandy	Sherry
Honey	Brown sugar
Ratafia biscuits	Macaroons
Redcurrant jelly	Indispensable – I seem to put it in everything
Stock	Stock cubes, yeast or vegetable extract
Vinegars	Wine, lemon juice, herbs

Instant Lunch or Supper

How often do you get landed unexpectedly with having to put a meal on the table in half an hour? Assuming your supermarket is not next door, I have concentrated on ingredients which you just might have available.

My formula for instant lunch or supper entertaining is to serve a meal in one dish and not fiddle around with different vegetables and sauces. Some dishes may need an accompanying salad, otherwise they are complete. I have also suggested a range of instant puddings but if you really want the easy life, cheese and some fresh fruit will be quite adequate.

THE SECRET COTTAGE

A perfect solution for transforming your Sunday lunch leftovers into an enchanting original dish. Cooked meat and vegetables are used as a filling for a hollowed-out cottage loaf. Little florets of broccoli and cauliflowers are then planted around the cottage garden.

SERVES 6

1 cottage loaf

melted butter

25 g/1 oz dripping

25 g/1 oz plain flour

300 ml/½ pint red wine

300 ml/½ pint boiling water with 1 stock cube (lamb or beef) dissolved in it

350 g/12 oz cooked lamb or beef, cut into strips

350 g/12 oz cooked potatoes, carrots and other vegetables, diced

FLAVOURINGS FOR LAMB

1 garlic clove

5 ml/1 tsp garam masala

15 ml/1 tbsp redcurrant jelly

5 ml/1 tsp mint sauce

15 ml/1 tbsp red wine vinegar

salt and pepper

FLAVOURINGS FOR BEEF

7.5 ml/1½ tsp prepared mustard

15 ml/1 tbsp apricot jam

15 ml/1 tbsp lemon juice

2.5 ml/½ tsp paprika

salt and pepper

225 g/8 oz broccoli, broken into florets

225 g/8 oz cauliflower, broken into florets

Remove the top knob from the loaf and hollow out the inside without cutting through the sides. (The discarded bread is ideal for making croûtons or breadcrumbs for another meal). Brush the loaf with a little melted butter and put on a baking sheet ready to fill later.

Set the oven at 200°C/400°F/gas 6.

Melt the dripping in a saucepan, then stir in the flour to make a roux. Cook the flour for 1 minute, gradually add the wine and stock. Boil for 3–5 minutes. I have suggested ingredients for flavouring lamb or beef but you can experiment with many others – see the section on gravies on page 109.

When the sauce is to your liking, add the meat and vegetables. Simmer until thoroughly heated. Pour the hot mixture into the prepared cottage loaf, replace the top knob and bake for 15 minutes. Cook the cauliflower and broccoli.

Transfer the loaf to a decorative round serving platter and arrange the vegetables alternately around the edge.

To serve, slice the loaf like a cake, spooning some of the casserole filling over each portion.

BAKED COD WITH FENNEL

A very economical recipe that successfully disguises frozen cod steaks and by combining them with fennel creates a flavoursome and interesting dish.

SERVES 6

margarine for greasing

6 (100 g/4 oz) frozen cod steaks

2 fennel bulbs, coarsely chopped

salt and pepper

600 ml/1 pint Greek yogurt

225 g/8 oz Cheddar cheese, grated

paprika

grated rind of 1 lemon

Grease an ovenproof dish. Set the oven at 200°C/400°F/gas 6.

Arrange the frozen cod steaks in the ovenproof dish. Scatter the fennel over the fish. Add salt and pepper to taste. Spoon the yogurt over the top and then cover with the grated cheese. Sprinkle with paprika and lemon rind. Bake for 25 minutes.

This dish is ready to serve directly from the oven although you may wish to drain off some of the fish juices.

SMOKED TROUT PATE

This is not a main course dish but I include it in this chapter because served with some cheese or charcuterie, it makes a perfectly satisfactory lunch without much trouble at all.

SERVES 6

1 smoked trout (or 2 fillets)

225 g/8 oz Philadelphia light cream cheese

15 ml/1 tbsp lemon juice

10 ml/2 tsp horseradish sauce

salt and pepper

30 ml/2 tbsp milk

GARNISH

black olives

red, yellow or green pepper

Take the fish off the bone and roughly flake it. Put all the ingredients into a food processor and process for a few seconds until smooth. Transfer to a serving dish and garnish with black olives and strips of sweet pepper.

Serve with fingers of pitta bread, celery, sweet peppers and carrots.

BACON AND ONION SOUFFLE

Although making a soufflé can hardly be considered as cheating, once you are brave enough to make one you will be delighted by how adaptable and delectable an instant meal it really is. In this recipe I use bacon, onion and Cheddar cheese but you can substitute all sorts of vegetables, fish, seafood or other cheeses and get some exciting results.

SERVES 6

1 onion, chopped

oil for frying

175 g/6 oz bacon, chopped

25 g/1 oz margarine

25 g/1 oz plain flour

150 ml/¼ pint milk

175 g/6 oz Cheddar cheese, grated

salt and pepper

5 ml/1 tsp Dijon mustard

6 eggs, separated

Set the oven at 190°C/375°F/gas 5.

Fry the onion gently in a little oil for 2–3 minutes, then add the bacon and cook together until tender. Transfer the mixture to a sieve to drain off the oil.

Melt the margarine in a large sauce-pan, stir in the flour and cook for 1 minute. Add the milk and bring to the boil, stirring rapidly. Add the cheese and continue to stir until smooth. Remove from the heat and add the mustard, with salt and pepper to taste. When the pan is cool enough to hold your hand on its side, stir in the egg yolks. Beat the egg whites until stiff, then fold into the sauce with a metal spoon. (It is a good idea to add half the whites, mix them in, then add the rest with as little folding as possible.)

Spoon a layer of the egg mixture into a 1.75-litre/3-pint soufflé dish, filling about a third of the dish. Cover with a layer of the onion and bacon mixture, then another layer of the egg mixture, the remaining onion and bacon, and a top layer of egg. Bake the soufflé for 30 minutes and serves immediately.

NOT FOR THE RUSSIANS – CHEAT'S BORTSCH WITH PIROSHKI

I say not for the Russians because I feel they would turn up their noses – genuine bortsch and authentic yeast-risen piroshki are much more effort than the average cheat is prepared to make but these versions are easy and effective.

SERVES 6

BORTSCH

25 g/1 oz margarine

1 small onion, sliced

25 g/1 oz plain flour

1.1 litres/2 pints boiling water with 3 chicken stock cubes dissolved in it

225 g/8 oz cooked beetroot, roughly chopped

salt and pepper

150 ml/5 fl oz soured cream

Melt the margarine in a large saucepan and cook the onion in it until soft. Stir in the flour and allow to cook before adding the stock slowly. Then add the beetroot to the mixture, bring to the boil and simmer for 5 minutes.

Purée the soup in a food processor until smooth. Alternatively, use a mouli-grinder. Reheat the soup, add salt and pepper to taste and stir in the soured cream.

PIROSHKI

oil for greasing

225 g/8 oz frozen puff pastry, thawed

50 g/2 oz cooked long-grain rice

1 hard-boiled egg, diced

6 spring onions, chopped

salt and pepper

ground cinnamon

egg wash

Grease a baking sheet and set the oven at 200°C/400°F/gas 6.

Roll out the puff pastry wafer thin. Using a 7.5-cm/3-inch cutter, cut into rounds.

Mix the rice, egg and spring onion together. Add salt, pepper and cinnamon to taste. Place a teaspoonful of this filling on to each pastry round, brush the edges of the pastry with water and fold them in two, pinching the joins together into a miniature pasty shape. Brush the piroshki with egg wash and bake for 10 minutes.

Serve hot with the bortsch.

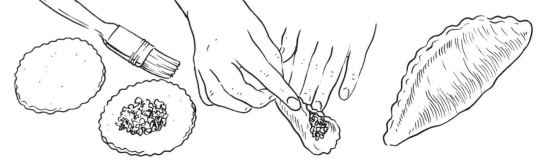

HEALTH FIEND'S STUFFED MARROW

A whole marrow stuffed with dried fruits and nuts, sitting on a bed of red cabbage. This autumnal dish of contrasting colours makes a wholesome and unusual vegetarian meal.

SERVES 6

1 green vegetable marrow
75 g/3 oz sage and onion stuffing
300 g/¹/₂ pint boiling water
15 g/¹/₂ oz butter
1 celery stick
1 carrot, diced
75 g/3 oz raisins
100 g/4 oz ready-to-eat dried apricots, chopped
100 g/4 oz hazelnuts
salt and pepper
lemon juice
1 small red cabbage
25 g/1 oz margarine
redcurrant jelly
red wine vinegar
225 g/8 oz fromage frais

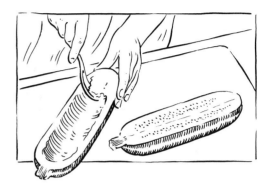

Set the oven at 200°C/400°/gas 6.

If the outer skin of the marrow seems tough, blanch it by simply pouring a kettle of boiling water over it and then cooling the skin under the cold tap. Halve the marrow lengthways and scoop out the centre pith and seeds.

Mix the stuffing with the boiling water and butter. Add the celery, carrot, raisins, half the apricots and half the hazelnuts (reserve the remainder to garnish the red cabbage). Add parsley, salt, pepper and lemon juice to taste.

Fill both halves of the marrow with the stuffing and sandwich them back together. Wrap the marrow loosely in foil leaving some room for it to swell. Bake for 40 minutes.

Core the red cabbage and slice it. Cook in boiling salted water for just 5 minutes and drain. Then sauté it in the margarine for about 10 minutes. I like it sweetened with redcurrant jelly, seasoned with plenty of salt and pepper and sprinkled with vinegar to restore its purple colour.

When you are ready to serve, drain the cabbage again, then make a nest of it on a serving platter. Scatter the reserved apricots and nuts on top. Unwrap the marrow and place it in the middle of the nest.

Sprinkle with parsley and serve a bowl of fromage frais to accompany the dish.

ROQUEFORT SALAD WITH CROUTONS AND WALNUTS

Another of my favourite one-dish meals is a huge bowl of a really tasty warm salad. This recipe is highly adaptable and can be based on any salad items or cheese you have available. Roquefort is particularly good but Stilton or Dolcelatte would give you a similar result.

SERVES 6

¼ loaf stale bread
oil for frying
50 g/2 oz walnuts, chopped
1 curly endive
1 radicchio
150 ml/¼ pint groundnut oil
150 ml/¼ pint walnut oil
1 garlic clove, crushed
175 g/6 oz Roquefort cheese
2 egg yolks
15 ml/1 tbsp lemon vinegar
salt and pepper

Remove the crusts from the bread and cut the loaf into small dice. Heat 1 cm/½ inch oil in a frying pan and fry the bread and chopped nuts together until golden brown. Drain on absorbent kitchen paper and set aside.

Prepare the endive and radicchio by tearing them into small tufts – this is much more effective than cutting with a knife.

Warm both oils in a saucepan with the garlic but do not allow this to get too hot. Grate or flake the Roquefort cheese into a mixing bowl, add the egg yolks and blend. Continue to blend while slowly adding the warm oil. Finally add the vinegar, with salt and pepper to taste.

If you don't want to serve the salad immediately, the dressing can be reheated by stirring in a bowl over a saucepan of simmering hot water. Pour the dressing over the salad leaves and toss while still warm. Sprinkle the croûtons and nuts over the salad and serve immediately.

STIR-FRY PRAWNS EN CROUTE

This is rather a fun main dish comprising of fish-shaped pastry cases filled with a stir-fry of prawns and crunchy vegetables.

SERVES 6

oil for greasing

350 g/12 oz frozen puff pastry, thawed

egg wash

30 ml/2 tbsp oil

1 garlic clove, crushed

1 red pepper, cored, seeded and cut into diamonds

1 green pepper, cored, seeded and cut into diamonds

1 (225 g/8 oz) can waterchestnuts, drained and halved

150 ml/¼ pint boiling water with ½ fish stock cube dissolved in it

100 ml/3½ fl oz dry sherry

15 ml/1 tbsp tomato ketchup

5 ml/1 tsp soy sauce

450 g/1 lb frozen peeled cooked prawns, thawed

15 ml/1 tbsp cornflour

GARNISH

1 round lettuce, shredded

12 radishes, cut into flowers

Oil a baking sheet and set the oven at 200°C/400°F/gas 6.

Roll out the pastry evenly to make about a 25-cm/10-inch square. Cut out simple shapes of one large fish and six small ones. (You don't have to be an artist – the more eccentric your fish shapes, the better.) With the tip of a pointed knife, score round each fish shape without cutting right through the pastry and leaving a border of about 1 cm/½ inch. Brush the pastry shapes with egg wash, place on the prepared baking sheet and bake for 10 minutes.

When the pastry is cooked, retrace the inner cuts and remove the inside 'lids' – you end up with fish-shaped vol-au-vent cases. Reduce the oven temperature to 160°C/325°F/gas 3.

Heat the oil in a frying pan or wok. Toss the garlic, peppers and waterchestnuts in the oil for a few moments. Add the fish stock, sherry, ketchup and soy sauce, bring to the boil and add salt and pepper to taste. Add the prawns to the mixture. When it returns to the boil, mix the cornflour with a little extra cold water and stir this into the pan to thicken the liquid.

Reheat the pastry cases for a few minutes, then spoon the stir-fry mixture into them. Arrange the filled fish on a dish and garnish with shredded lettuce and radish flowers.

Serve each guest with a slice of the large fish and one small fish.

ARTICHOKE CUPS WITH HAM AND GRUYERE

These yummy little stuffed artichoke hearts can be used as a main lunch or supper dish, a starter or as a fine partner for grilled meats or fish.

SERVES 6

2 (200 g/7 oz) cans artichoke hearts, drained

100 g/4 oz smoked ham, diced

1 (150 g/5 oz) can tomatoes, drained

½ garlic clove, crushed

salt and pepper

100 g/4 oz Gruyère cheese, grated

Set the oven at 220°C/425°F/gas 7.

With your thumbs re-shape the artichoke hearts into cups. Arrange in an ovenproof dish, cutting a little off the base if necessary for them to sit upright.

Mix the ham with the tomato and garlic with salt and pepper to taste. Spoon this into each artichoke cup. Sprinkle the grated cheese over the top and bake for 10–15 minutes. Serve hot with a crisp dressed salad.

POTATO AND TUNA FISH GRATIN

Layers of sliced potato, tuna fish and onion baked in the oven with a topping of melted cheese . . . not exotic but very appetizing.

SERVES 6

450 g/1 lb old potatoes, thinly sliced

1 (225 g/8 oz) can tuna fish, well drained and flaked

1 onion, sliced

2 garlic cloves, crushed

salt and pepper

2 eggs

450 ml/¾ pint milk

75 g/3 oz Cheddar cheese, grated

75 g/3 oz red Leicester cheese, grated

chopped parsley, to garnish

Set the oven at 220°C/425°F/gas 7.

Put an even layer of the potatoes on the bottom of an ovenproof dish. Cover with half the tuna fish and half the onion. Add half the garlic and plenty of salt and pepper. Layer again with potatoes, then the remaining tuna fish, onion and garlic. Add more salt and pepper. Top with a final layer of potatoes. Mix the milk and eggs together, then pour over so it drains down into the layers. Sprinkle the two cheeses on top, either randomly or in strips. Bake for 1 hour.

Keep warm until required and serve sprinkled with parsley.

Spinach and Mushroom Roulade

A roulade is a sort of flattened soufflé – cooked and then rolled up with a filling inside. Rather like a soufflé, once you have mastered the simple technique, it is a highly adaptable dish which only takes minutes to make. In this recipe I have chosen a spinach roulade with a mushroom filling but the alternatives are innumerable. You could try fish, broccoli or tomato roulades. Then there are sweet roulades of chocolate or nuts – the sky is the limit but let's perfect this simple spinach one first.

SERVES 6

oil for greasing

450 g/1 lb frozen spinach (about 225 g/8 oz when drained)

6 eggs, separated

salt and pepper

ground nutmeg

30 ml/2 tbsp grated Parmesan cheese

FILLING

450 g/1 lb mushrooms, chopped

25 g/1 oz margarine

30 ml/2 tbsp Greek yogurt

GARNISH

watercress

cherry tomatoes

Oil a roulade or Swiss roll tin and line with non-stick baking parchment. Set the oven at 200°C/400°F/gas 6.

Drain the spinach really well, pressing or squeezing the water out of it. In a bowl mix the spinach, egg yolks and plenty of salt, pepper and nutmeg. Whisk the egg whites in a separate bowl until stiff. Fold the whites into the spinach mixture, using a metal spoon and the minimum of stirring. Spoon the mixture into the prepared tin, sprinkle with the Parmesan and bake for 15 minutes.

Meanwhile prepare the filling by gently sautéing the mushrooms in the margarine for 4–5 minutes. Add salt and pepper and drain off the liquid. Leave to cool, then mix with the yogurt.

Allow the roulade to cool slightly before turning it out on to a sheet of greaseproof paper. The baking parchment will easily peel off the back. Spread the filling on to the roulade. Now the tricky bit: picking up one edge of the greaseproof paper with both hands, make a first tight tuck in the roulade, then roll it up firmly like a Swiss roll. Transfer to a large plate, remove the greaseproof paper and garnish with watercress and cherry tomatoes. A tomato coulis (page 59) would go well with it.

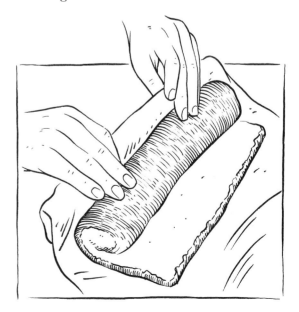

CHICKEN GOUGERE

I must confess that I have no short-cut method for making a gougère. I include it, however, because it is quite the most successful lunch or supper dish I know and you really must try it. Savoury choux pastry is arranged in a ring and then filled with any sort of meat, fish or vegetable mixture. The two are cooked together making a lovely gunge where they meet.

SERVES 6

butter for greasing

150 ml/¼ pint water

50 g/2 oz butter, diced

65 g/2½ oz plain flour

2 eggs

50 g/2 oz Cheddar cheese, grated

salt

cayenne pepper

25 g/1 oz Parmesan cheese, grated

chopped parsley, to garnish

FILLING

350 g/12 oz cooked chicken

75 ml/3 fl oz tomato chutney

300 ml/10 fl oz natural yogurt

1 (150 g/5 oz) can sweetcorn, drained

pepper

Butter an ovenproof dish. Set the oven at 200°C/400°F/gas 6.

Boil the water and butter together until they bubble up in the saucepan. Remove from the heat and immediately shoot in the flour (that lovely expression means all at once – double quick – chop chop). Beat the mixture until quite smooth. Allow to cool slightly, then beat the mixture again for 2–3 minutes while gradually adding the eggs. It should end up soft and shiny. Stir in the Cheddar cheese. Add salt and cayenne to taste. Set aside while preparing the filling.

Cut the chicken into small strips and mix with the tomato chutney, yogurt and sweetcorn. Add salt and pepper to taste.

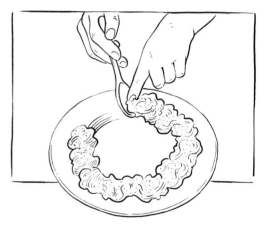

Spoon the gougère mixture around the edge of the prepared dish in a ring shape. This need not be very neat as long as you make a complete ring. Spoon the filling into the centre and sprinkle the Parmesan cheese over the gougère ring. Bake for 35 minutes. Garnish with chopped parsley and serve.

CREME FRAMBOISE

Yogurt, cream and raspberries transformed into an exquisite little dish which I make again and again. The demerara sugar crystals half-dissolve in the refrigerator creating a special crunchy topping.

SERVES 6

300 ml/10 fl oz double cream

1 (400 g/14 oz) can raspberries, drained

300 ml/10 fl oz plain yogurt

30 ml/2 tbsp caster sugar

30 ml/2 tbsp lemon juice

about 75 g/3 oz demerara sugar

Whip the cream to a folding consistency. Mix in the raspberries and yogurt. Add the caster sugar and lemon juice, then spoon the mixture into a serving dish.

Cover the top of the mixture with a generous layer of demerara sugar. Chill for 3–4 hours.

PEARS BELLE HELENE

A classic dish which can be easily recreated from a can of pears, a tub of vanilla ice cream and a jar of chocolate spread. Fresh pears can of course be used when they are in season.

SERVES 6

2 (425 g/15 oz) cans pears, drained

600 ml/1 pint vanilla ice cream

60 ml/4 tbsp chocolate spread

15 ml/1 tbsp boiling water

1 small chocolate flake bar, crushed

Arrange the pear halves in a circle on a round serving dish. Scoop the ice cream into small balls and pile these in the centre of the pears.

Mix the chocolate spread with the boiling water and pour over each pear. Scatter the chocolate flakes over the ice cream and serve.

SNOW ROLL

Is it meringue? Is it pavlova or marshmallow? Whatever it is, it's incredibly gooey, and popular with any sweet tooth – young or old.

SERVES 6

oil for greasing

5 egg whites

225 g/8 oz caster sugar

5 ml/1 tsp white wine vinegar

5 ml/1 tsp vanilla essence

15 ml/1 tbsp cornflour

icing sugar

FILLING

300 ml/10 fl oz double cream

175 g/6 oz seedless grapes

DECORATION

seedless grapes or other fresh fruit

icing sugar

Oil a roulade or Swiss roll tin and line it with non-stick baking parchment. Set the oven at 180°C/350°F/gas 4.

Whisk the egg whites until they are very stiff, then continue to beat while adding the caster sugar a spoonful at a time. Add the vinegar, vanilla essence and cornflour and mix thoroughly. Spoon the mixture into the prepared tin and spread it out, right to the edges. Bake for 15 minutes – the snow will rise but when it cools, it will fall a little.

Dust a large sheet of greaseproof paper with icing sugar and turn the snow on to it. Whip the cream and mix in the grapes. Spread the mixture on to the snow and then using the paper to help you, gently roll it up.

Transfer to a serving plate and decorate with chosen fruit and extra icing sugar.

OLDE ENGLISH BAKED APPLES

'Just like mother used to make,' only rather easier. Although I profess to know nothing about microwave ovens, this particular recipe works extremely well in one. You need to score the skin of the apples right round the circumference and then prepare as below. Microwave on High for 4 minutes.

SERVES 6

6 Bramley apples

about 225 g/8 oz mincemeat

15 g/½ oz butter

Set the oven at 180°C/350°F/gas 4.

Make a 2.5-cm/1-inch hole in the centre of each apple and remove the core. Put the apples in an ovenproof dish and spoon some mincemeat into the centre of each. Put a knob of butter on top of each apple and a little water in the base of the dish. Bake for 30 minutes.

Serve hot with single cream or custard.

LEMON TART

An effective little disguise which I forbid you to give away! It will serve you for years if you don't.

SERVES 6

oil for greasing

225 g/8 oz frozen shortcrust pastry, thawed

350 g/12 oz lemon curd

2 eggs, lightly beaten

icing sugar

Oil a 18-cm/7-inch flan tin lightly. Set the oven at 180°C/350°F/gas 4.

Roll out the pastry evenly and fit it into the prepared flan tin. To help those of you who are less experienced with pastry, remember that, it is important after cutting away the excess, to press the pastry up above the sides of the tin to allow for shrinkage. This is called 'knocking it up' which should make it easy to remember. Prick the base of the pastry all over with a fork.

Mix the lemon curd with the eggs and pour the mixture into the pastry case. Bake for 25 minutes. When the tart comes out of the oven dust it immediately with icing sugar and place it under a hot grill to caramelize the top. The tart can then be kept waiting but should be served warm.

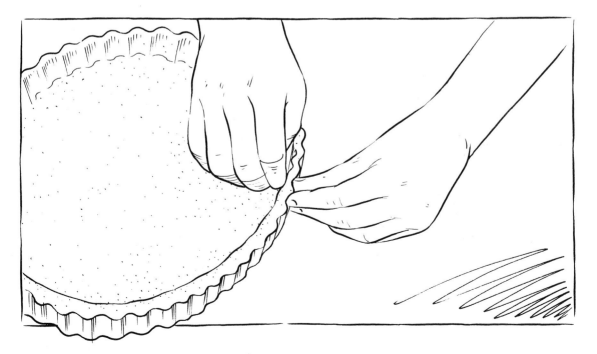

PLUM FOOL

This traditional recipe uses ready-made custard to make life easy. The addition of orange enhances the flavour of the plums.

SERVES 6

900 g/2 lb plums, halved and stoned

45 ml/3 tbsp soft light brown sugar

150 ml/¼ pint water

zest and juice of 1 orange

300 ml/½ pint carton thick custard

150 ml/5 fl oz whipping cream, lightly whipped

DECORATION

slices of uncooked plums

fresh mint leaves

Put the plums in a saucepan with the sugar and water and simmer for about 10 minutes until very soft. Add the orange zest and juice and purée in a blender. Alternatively, use a mouli-grinder. Mix the purée with the custard and cream, pour into a serving dish and chill for 3–4 hours.

Decorate with slices of uncooked plums and mint leaves.

THE ULTIMATE CHOCOLATE MOUSSE

This totally self-indulgent pudding is designed to give the cook as much finger-licking and bowl-scraping as possible – so you feel really sick when you have finished making it!

SERVES 6

175 g/6 oz plain chocolate

45 ml/3 tbsp strong black coffee

15 ml/1 tbsp brandy

10 ml/2 tsp caster sugar

3 eggs, separated

double or whipping cream, to decorate (optional)

Put the chocolate, brandy and sugar in a small saucepan and melt it over a very gentle heat stirring until it is completely smooth. Don't let the mixture boil. While it is hot stir in the egg yolks one at a time. Allow to cool.

Whisk the egg whites in a dry bowl until stiff. Fold the whites into the chocolate mixture and transfer to a serving dish. Chill for 3–4 hours before serving. Decorate with piped whipped cream, if used.

Lemon Tart and Olde English Baked Apple

Potato and Tuna Fish Gratin with Roquefort Salad

Iced Melon and Mint Soup, Mosaic of Fishes, Brandy-snap Baskets with Sorbet
and Fresh Fruits

Borscht with Piroshki (don't tell the Russians!)

Mexican Chicken and Avocado

Brioches of Pork and Apple, with carrots, cauliflower and broccoli

Plateau d'été, with dips

Bacon and Onion Soufflé

HONEYED FRUIT KEBABS

Prepared fruits coated in honey and sherry served piping hot . . . this is a marvellously different way of presenting fresh fruit which can be adapted for almost any fruit you have available.

SERVES 6

4 firm bananas

3 nectarines

225 g/8 oz fresh black cherries, stalks discarded

45 ml/3 tbsp thick honey

15 ml/1 tbsp sherry

5 ml/1 tsp lemon juice

pinch of ground cinnamon

pinch of ground cloves

Set the grill at hot.

Slice the bananas into 2.5-cm/1-inch lengths. Cut the nectarines into eighths, discarding the stones. Skewer the fruits on to 12 wooden or metal kebab sticks, alternating the colours.

Mix the honey, sherry, lemon juice and spices together. Arrange the kebabs in a shallow tin and pour the honey mixture over. Cook under the grill for 3–4 minutes, turning the kebabs occasionally and recoating them with the honey mixture. Serve immediately.

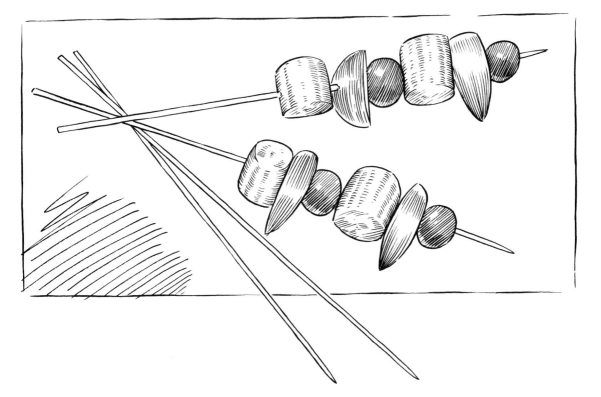

Dinner Party Ideas

Easy to make, original, beautifully presented and tasting delicious – not a lot to ask?
A cheat's first priority for a dinner party is to make sure he or she is going to be able to relax and enjoy it. You don't want just to be the cook in the kitchen and with this in mind here are various guidelines to help you.

Choose relatively simple dishes which don't all require last-minute attention.

Unless you love experimenting, select recipes which you understand and leave the breaking of new ground to your 'dinner for two'.

Prepare all the ingredients you can in advance; even some garnishes and decorations can be made.

Set your dining-room with everything ready – table laid, wines open, water available, even the coffee service set out.

Finally, wash up all your utensils and tidy the kitchen before the dinner party begins.

I have presented the recipes in this chapter as ten complete three-course menus although you can adapt them, swap them or combine dishes with others of your own. The menus, however, are intended to show you how to balance your meal. Colour, texture, content, style and shape are all important and just because we are going to cheat does not mean your meal should be anything less than perfect.

MIDSUMMER NIGHT

Plateau d'Eté

Carré d'Agneau

Beaumes-de-Venise Syllabub with Strawberries and Black Grapes

This menu can be used at many times of the year but it has the special magic of midsummer. It also introduces another weapon in the cheat's arsenal – the use of fancy French names for the simplest of dishes!

PLATEAU D'ETE

A large raised platter set in the centre of your table overflowing with seafood
and summer vegetables. Although simple to prepare this dish will never fail to
enthral your guests. It can be easily adapted to use many different ingredients
such as quail's eggs, langoustine or smoked salmon.

SERVES 6

2 globe artichokes, stalks trimmed

450 g/1 lb asparagus, trimmed

salt

1 onion, sliced

lemon juice

450 g/1lb mussels

1 melon

18 whole cooked king prawns

18 whole cooked crab claws

100 g/4 oz cherry tomatoes

100 g/4 oz white mushrooms

1 bunch radishes

WATERCRESS MAYONNAISE

1 bunch watercress, finely chopped

150 ml/¼ pint mayonnaise

TSATSIKI

¼ cucumber, peeled and grated

150 ml/5 fl oz natural yogurt

crushed garlic

salt and pepper

Cook the artichokes in boiling salted
water for 30 minutes. Drain and leave to
cool. Cook the asparagus in boiling salted
water for about 10 minutes until tender.
Drain and immediately cool the asparagus
under the cold tap.

Put about 2.5 cm/1 inch water in the
bottom of a deep saucepan with the
onion and a little lemon juice. Add the
mussels and simmer for 5 minutes or
until the mussels are open. Discard any
that remain closed. Drain and cool.

Cut the melon into narrow boat-shaped
slices and remove the seeds.

Arrange all the different ingredients in
clusters – separate but overlapping – on
the platter. The platter itself needs to be
raised on the table on a little stand – an
inverted terracotta flower pot is ideal
provided it doesn't scratch the table.

To make the watercress mayonnaise, just
whisk the watercress into the mayonnaise,
perhaps adding some more salt and
pepper.

To make the tsatsiki, drain the cucumber
and mix with the yogurt, garlic, salt and
pepper.

These sauces should be served in little
dishes placed around the table.

CARRE D'AGNEAU

This sounds very grand but it is easy to cook and carve. It makes a delicious main course served with vegetables or salad. Ask a butcher or look in your supermarket for 'French trimmed' rack of lamb (all this means is the fat is left on the meat but trimmed off the bones).

SERVES 6

3–4 'French trimmed' whole racks of lamb (allow 3 cutlets per person)

150 ml/¼ pint red wine

150 ml/¼ pint water

15 ml/1 tbsp redcurrant jelly

fresh rosemary

1 garlic clove, crushed

15 ml/1 tbsp cornflour mixed with cold water

GARNISH

watercress

nasturtium flowers

Set the oven at 220°C/425°F/gas 7 for 20 minutes.

Roast the lamb for 20 minutes. Remove from the oven. Pour the wine, water and redcurrant jelly around the joint and sprinkle rosemary and garlic on top. Return to the oven for a further 15 minutes.

The meat can now be kept warm resting in its liquid for up to 30 minutes. When ready to serve, remove the meat, reboil the liquid and stir in the cornflour.

Carve the meat down between each bone and arrange on a serving platter. Garnish with watercress and nasturtiums and serve the sauce separately.

BEAUMES-DE-VENISE SYLLABUB WITH FRESH STRAWBERRIES AND BLACK GRAPES

A stunning and virtually instant summer dessert full of delicious calories.

SERVES 6

450 ml/15 fl oz double cream

100 ml/3½ fl oz Beaumes-de-Venise or other muscat dessert wine

150 g/5 oz caster sugar

grated zest of 1 lemon

450 g/1 lb seedless black grapes, stalks removed

450 g/1 lb fresh strawberries, hulled

15 ml/1 tbsp icing sugar

mint leaves

Put the cream, wine, sugar and lemon zest in a mixing bowl and beat preferably with an electric whisk until just firm.

Spoon the mixture into a serving bowl. Scatter the fruits on top. Dust with the icing sugar and decorate with a few mint leaves tucked in among the fruits.

CHEAT'S CORDON BLEU

Quenelles of Country Pâté with Cumberland Sauce

Sauté of Beef Stroganoff

Peaches à la Diable

If you possess a cordon bleu cook book, I recommend you use it as a prop laid open at some highly technical page while you produce this deceptively easy meal.

QUENELLES OF COUNTRY PATE WITH CUMBERLAND SAUCE

Transform a supermarket pâté into something that tastes homemade and looks cordon bleu.

SERVES 6

225 g/8 oz smooth pâté
25 g/1 oz gherkins, chopped
25 g/1 oz capers, chopped
30 ml/2 tbsp cooking brandy
salt and pepper

GARNISH

12 fresh bay leaves
6 cherry tomatoes

CUMBERLAND SAUCE

60 ml/4 tbsp redcurrant jelly
grated rind and juice of 1 orange
100 ml/3½ fl oz port
juice of 1 lemon

Put the pâté, gherkins, capers and brandy, with salt and pepper to taste, in a bowl and mix well. Then with two dessert-spoons mould the pâté into an oval or 'quenelle' shape by passing a spoonful from one spoon to the other. Arrange two quenelles on each plate in a 'V' formation and garnish with bay leaves and a tomato star at the base.

A tomato star sounds much more tricky than it is – simply cut each tomato into quarters and then eighths but without cutting the bottom skin all the way through. The eight sections should then flop open but be held symmetrically at the base.

To make Cumberland sauce, heat the redcurrant jelly until dissolved and add the orange rind. Stir in the port, and orange and lemon juices. Leave to cool. Pour a little on to each pâté plate just before serving.

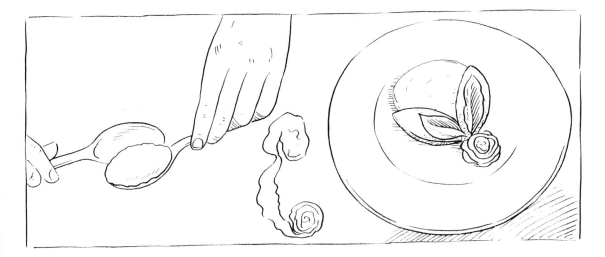

SAUTE OF BEEF STROGANOFF

Traditional recipes for stroganoff require very expensive fillet steak and a great deal of 'flambé' and washing up! This one-stage cooking formula may not give you exactly the same result but I wonder who will know the difference. To accompany I recommend a mixture of long-grain and brown rice and a crisp green salad.

SERVES 6

1.1 kg/2½ lb chuck steak (good quality – not stewing steak)
50 g/2 oz dripping or lard
1 onion, chopped
50 g/2 oz plain flour
1 (200 g/7½ oz) can concentrated beef consommé
450 ml/¾ pint water
20 g/¾ oz dried mushrooms
1 garlic clove, crushed
15 ml/1 tbsp tomato purée
salt and pepper
150 ml/5 fl oz soured cream
chopped parsley, to garnish

Trim any gristle and most of the fat from the steak – the prepared weight should be about 900 g/2 lb. Cut the steak into neat strips about 4 cm/1½ inches long and the thickness of a pen.

Melt the dripping or lard in a large heavy-bottomed pan and fry the onion for 1 minute. Then add the steak and seal this in the dripping. Spoon in the flour, stirring rapidly, and when blended pour in the water and consommé.

Add the dried mushrooms, garlic and tomato purée, with salt and pepper to taste. Bring to the boil and simmer gently for about 30 minutes until the beef is tender.

This dish will reheat quite happily on the hob. Stir in the soured cream just before serving on a bed of rice. Sprinkle with chopped parsley.

PEACHES A LA DIABLE

Baked peaches with an almond brandy filling.

SERVES 6

6 firm peaches or nectarines, halved and stoned
175 g/6 oz almond ratafia biscuits
100 ml/3½ fl oz brandy
about 45 ml/3 tbsp soft light brown sugar

Set the oven at 220°C/425°F/gas 7.

Lay the peaches or nectarines in an ovenproof dish cut-side up. Arrange a line of 3 ratafia biscuits in the centre of each half and spoon the brandy on top. Cover with a generous layer of brown sugar and bake for about 5 minutes.

Serve immediately with lashings of whipped cream (very cordon bleu!).

THE HELPFUL BAKER

Watercress and Almond Soup

Brioche of Pork and Apple

Butterscotch Flan

Why do we always assume that there must be potatoes or at least rice or pasta to accompany a main course? Our staple diet is bread and if you use it wisely, a good baker will do all the work for you.

WATERCRESS AND ALMOND SOUP

Pale green in colour with the fresh peppery flavour of watercress offset by the nutty body of ground almonds.

SERVES 6

15 g/½ oz margarine
225 g/8 oz potatoes, diced
2 bunches watercress
grated rind of 1 lemon
100 g/4 oz ground almonds
600 ml/1 pint boiling water with 1 chicken stock cube dissolved in it
600 ml/1 pint milk
salt and pepper

Melt the margarine in a large saucepan and toss the potatoes, one bunch of watercress, lemon rind and almonds in it for about 1 minute. Add the stock and milk. Bring to the boil and simmer for 20 minutes. When cooked purée in a food processor until smooth. Alternatively, use a mouli-grinder. Add salt and pepper to taste.

The soup can now be left and reheated when needed. Just before serving chop the remaining bunch of watercress finely and add to the soup to finish.

BRIOCHES OF APPLE AND PORK

Most good bakers will make brioches and even if these are not displayed regularly, with advance notice they will be delighted to fulfil your request. Frankly I do not think this dish needs anything but colourful lightly boiled vegetables served with it.

SERVES 6

50 g/2 oz margarine
900 g/2 lb pork tenderloin, trimmed
1 large onion, sliced into rings
50 g/2 oz plain flour
600 ml/1 pint cider
30 ml/2 tbsp cider vinegar
15 ml/1 tbsp soft dark brown sugar
15 ml/1 tbsp lemon juice
salt and pepper
1 red apple, cored and sliced (not peeled)
1 green apple, cored and sliced (not peeled)
6 individual brioches
chopped parsley, to garnish

Melt the margarine in a large frying pan and sauté the tenderloin until sealed all over. Remove the meat, add the chopped onion to the fat and fry until soft. Stir in

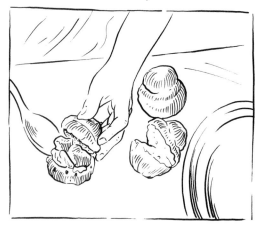

the flour to make a roux. Let the flour cook for 1 minute, then add the cider, vinegar, sugar and lemon juice. (If you do this too quickly and your sauce goes lumpy, don't panic, just keep stirring and it will smooth out.) Add plenty of salt and pepper.

Slice the tenderloin crossways into small rondelles, put these into the sauce and cook for 10 minutes. Then, add the sliced apples and cook for a further 5 minutes. Leave off the heat until just before serving.

Set the oven at 200°C/400°F/gas 6.

Just before serving, reheat the pork mixture and warm the brioches in the oven. Cut the brioches open on one side and with a perforated spoon put a good dollop of the meat mixture into each.

Arrange them on a serving platter and spoon more of the filling and sauce around them. Sprinkle with chopped parsley.

BUTTERSCOTCH FLAN

Did you know that by boiling a can of condensed milk you can turn it into the most delicious thick butterscotch sauce? This highly fattening and self-indulgent dessert takes full advantage of this fact.

SERVES 6

oil for greasing	
1 (225 g/8 oz) can condensed milk	
150 g/5 oz digestive biscuits, crumbled	
grated rind and juice of 1 orange	
50 g/2 oz butter, melted	
300 ml/10 fl oz double cream	
1 chocolate flake bar, crushed	

Put the sealed can of condensed milk in a saucepan of water and boil gently for 2 hours, making sure it does not boil dry. If you like this dessert, you can do several cans at once and then keep them in the store cupboard marked 'butterscotch'.

Oil a 25-cm/10-inch loose-bottomed flan tin thoroughly and line with a circle of greaseproof paper.

Mix the crumbled biscuits with the grated orange rind (not the juice) and melted butter. Press the mixture into the prepared flan tin. Leave to set.

Empty the can of butterscotch on to the biscuit base and spread it evenly. Whip the double cream to a firm but not dry consistency. Add the orange juice. Spoon this mixture over the butterscotch and spread evenly.

Remove from the flan tin by sliding a palette knife under the biscuit base. Transfer to an attractive round plate and scatter crushed chocolate flake on top.

CELEBRATION SPLASH

Iced Melon and Mint Soup

Mosaic of Fishes
with Tarragon Butter Sauce

Brandy-snap Baskets
with Sorbet and Fresh Fruits

A real special occasion menu which will impress your guests with your culinary talents as much as delight them with the food.

ICED MELON AND MINT SOUP

These two flavours complement each other beautifully and make a fresh and tantalizing starter.

SERVES 6

40 g/1½ oz margarine

40 g/1½ oz plain flour

1 ripe Ogen or Galia melon, peeled, seeds removed and roughly chopped

2 shallots, chopped

½ bunch fresh mint, chopped

1.1 litres/2 pints water

2 chicken stock cubes, crumbled

150 ml/5 fl oz crème fraîche

salt and pepper

GARNISH

crème fraîche

small mint leaves

Rub the margarine and flour together to make beurre manié.

Put the melon, shallots and half the chopped mint in a saucepan with the water and stock cubes. Simmer for 10 minutes. Whisk in the beurre manié and cook for a further 5 minutes.

Purée in a food processor in two lots until smooth. Alternatively, use a mouli-grinder.

Finally, stir in the crème fraîche and the remaining chopped mint. Add salt and pepper to taste. Chill for 3–4 hours.

Garnish each portion with an additional swirl of crème fraîche and a mint leaf.

TARRAGON BUTTER SAUCE

SERVES 6

225 g/8 oz unsalted butter

60 ml/4 tbsp tarragon vinegar

15 ml/1 tbsp caster sugar

5 ml/1 tsp salt

150 ml/5 fl oz crème fraîche

freshly ground black pepper

Melt the butter gently in a saucepan over a low heat, stirring all the time and being careful not to let it boil. When completely melted, add the vinegar, sugar and salt, then whisk like mad until your arm aches and the mixture is paler.

Stir in the crème fraîche with pepper to taste and keep in a warm (not hot) place until required.

MOSAIC OF FISHES

This recipe will appear to be very sophisticated and is so effective no one will believe how simple it is to achieve. Ask your fishmonger to help you by filleting and skinning the fish. To accompany I recommend boiled new potatoes and Tarragon Butter Sauce (page 53).

SERVES 6

1 (450 g/1 lb) salmon fillet, about 20 cm/8 inches long

1 (450 g/1 lb) halibut fillet, about 20 cm/8 inches long

salt and pepper

225 g/8 oz large spinach or Swiss chard leaves

1 bunch tarragon, chopped

Set the oven at 160°C/325°F/gas 3.

Cut each of the fillets lengthways into three so you now have six long strips of fish. Lay these in a shallow roasting tin with 1 cm/½ inch of salted water, cover with foil and poach gently for 10 minutes in the oven. Drain the hot liquid immediately from the fish.

Meanwhile blanch the spinach or Swiss chard leaves by plunging them into boiling water, then draining and chilling them in cold water.

Lay the spinach or Swiss chard leaves out on a work surface overlapping as shown to make a rectangle about 25 cm/10 inches long and 20 cm/8 inches wide. Remove any large stalks if necessary.

Arrange the strips of fish in alternate colours lengthways on the leaves and sprinkle chopped tarragon, salt and pepper in between them. Then lap the spinach over the fish and make as tightly rolled parcel as possible. (At this stage I have had the dish referred to as a 'big green slug'!) It can now be left cold until ready for dinner.

Set the oven at 160°C/325°F/gas 3. Put the parcel on a greased baking sheet, cover with foil and reheat for 15 minutes.

Serve by slicing crossways and revealing the 'mosaic' of fishes in a frame of green spinach – no longer a slug at all!

BRANDY-SNAP BASKETS WITH SORBET AND FRESH FRUITS

A real cheat recipe using ordinary packet brandy-snaps and remoulding them into little baskets to fill with sorbet and fruit.

SERVES 6

oil for greasing

175 g/6 oz large curl brandy-snaps

500 ml/17 fl oz lemon or orange sorbet

225 g/8 oz strawberries, sliced

100 g/4 oz blueberries (optional)

1 (225 g/8 oz) can raspberries

6 flowers, to decorate

Oil a baking sheet. Set the oven at 180°C/350°F/gas 4.

Put the brandy-snaps on the prepared baking sheet and warm in the oven for 2–3 minutes. The brandy-snaps will flatten out and as soon as they have done so, remove them from the baking sheet with a palette knife and mould them over the top of an orange or apple to form baskets.

When cold, fill each basket with sorbet and top with sliced strawberries and blueberries, if used. Purée the raspberries to make a little sauce. Put the baskets on individual plates and decorate with the sauce and fresh flowers.

VEGETARIAN FEASTING

Les Petits Cadeaux

Broccoli Soufflé
with Onion and Tomato Coulis

Baked Brie

It is always assumed that vegetarian food will be boringly good for you and incredibly dull. Now although I am a dedicated carnivore, I would dispute this and I think this menu is as tempting as any meat and two veg.

LES PETITS CADEAUX

Miniature parcels of filo pastry containing different spicy fillings on a bed of continental lettuces. You can make this dish with any number of fillings including smoked fishes, cheeses and poultry. The three different fillings, however, are quite fun when your guests explore their 'petits cadeaux' to see what is inside. The filo pastry is ready-made and surprisingly easy to use.

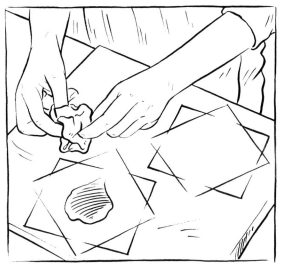

SERVES 6

butter for greasing
100 g/ 4 oz mushrooms, chopped
5 ml/1 tsp coriander seeds
1 garlic clove, crushed
salt and pepper
50 g/2 oz frozen spinach, thawed
mixed spice
salt and pepper
100 g/4 oz mango chutney
cayenne pepper
1 (225 g/8 oz) packet filo pastry
25 g/1 oz butter, melted
½ curly endive
1 radicchio
1 lollo rosso
30 ml/ 2 tbsp lemon juice
45 ml/3 tbsp olive oil
salt and pepper

Butter a baking sheet. Set the oven at 180°C/350°F/gas 4.

Prepare the three fillings. Put the mushrooms in a saucepan and sweat lightly in their own juices with the coriander seeds, garlic, salt and pepper. Dry the spinach by squeezing in a cloth and then add plenty of mixed spices, salt and pepper. Chop up the mango chutney if it has any large pieces and add cayenne.

Unroll the first sheet of filo carefully and lay it out on a work surface (keep the others under a damp tea-towel to prevent them drying out). From this sheet cut two 10-cm/4-inch squares. Lay one square on top of another at an angle so you make an eight-pointed star.

Put a spoonful of one of the fillings in the centre, then gather up all the sides and pinch them together like a little money bag. The pastry should stick but if it is very dry and springs open, just moisten your fingers lightly with water and squeeze it shut.

Make up three parcels per person (one of each filling) and then put them on the prepared baking sheet and dab a little melted butter on each. Bake the filo parcels for 10 minutes.

Tear the lettuces into tufts. Dress them generously with lemon juice, oil, salt and pepper and casually arrange on individual plates.

Put three parcels on each plate and serve.

BROCCOLI SOUFFLE

Make a soufflé for the main course of a dinner party – I can hear your dismayed
cry. What so few people realize is that a soufflé mixture can be entirely prepared
in advance as long as it is refrigerated from the moment it is made until it is
cooked. Just put it in the oven as your guests sit down and have an uninterrupted
35 minutes to serve, eat and clear the starter.

SERVES 6

450 g/1 lb fresh broccoli
25 g/1 oz margarine
15 ml/1 tbsp plain flour
150 ml/¼ pint milk
45 ml/3 tbsp grated Parmesan cheese
15 ml/1 tbsp lemon juice
salt and pepper
ground nutmeg
4 eggs, separated

Cook the broccoli. Then drain it
thoroughly and purée it in a food processor or blender.

In a large saucepan melt the margarine
and add the flour, stirring constantly.
Cook for 1 minute, then add the milk and
bring to the boil. Remove from the heat.
Stir in the broccoli purée, Parmesan
cheese, lemon juice and plenty of salt,
pepper and nutmeg (the taste is always
less pronounced in a soufflé when it is
cooked). When the mixture has cooled
slightly, stir in the egg yolks.

Whisk the egg whites in a clean bowl
until stiff. Using a metal spoon, fold the
egg whites into the broccoli mixture
lightly and carefully ladle into a 1.1-litre/
2-pint soufflé dish. Refrigerate for up to
2 hours.

Set the oven at 200°C/400°F/gas 6.
Bake the soufflé for 35 minutes.

ONION AND TOMATO COULIS

For many dishes I would recommend that you make this sauce quite spicy but so as not to overwhelm the soufflé, you must be cautious this time.

SERVES 6

oil for frying

1 large onion, chopped

1 (425 g/15 oz) can tomatoes

125 ml/4 fl oz red wine

½ garlic clove, crushed

salt and pepper

caster sugar

Tabasco

dried mixed herbs

Heat the oil in a saucepan and gently fry the onion until soft. Add the tomatoes, red wine and garlic, with salt, pepper, sugar, Tabasco and dried mixed herbs to taste. Simmer for 5 minutes. Purée in a food processor. Reheat just before serving.

BAKED BRIE

Any number of delicious desserts could be included in this menu but baked Brie with fresh fruit is my choice.

SERVES 6

¼ whole Brie (not too ripe)

1 egg, beaten

cornflour

oil for cooking

3 firm but ripe pears, quartered and pips removed

3 large dark plums, quartered and stones removed

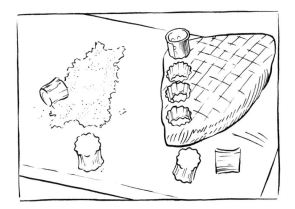

Set the oven at 220°C/425°F/gas 7.

Using a 4-cm/1½-inch pastry cutter, cut out 12 rounds of Brie. Carefully roll the sides in the beaten egg and then in cornflour so they look like whole miniature cheeses.

Heat a little oil in a pan and gently cook the mini Bries to seal the edges. Put the cheeses on a baking sheet and bake for 5 minutes before serving.

Make two cuts down each quartered pear and plum, leaving one end uncut so you can 'fan' the fruit. Arrange the pears and plums alternately in a ring on a serving platter and place the hot Bries in the centre.

JELLY AND ICE CREAM WITH A BIT IN THE MIDDLE

Seafood Chartreuse

Breast of Turkey with Norwegian Goat's Cheese

Pineapple and Cointreau Ice Cream

Anyone who claims a balanced menu can start with a jelly, serve meat and cheese together in the middle, then end on ice cream, must be a little mad. However, if you will join in the madness, I think you will have some fun and win appreciation for this meal.

SEAFOOD CHARTREUSE

A ring of spicy tomato jelly filled with seafood salad. This colourful starter will make a centre-piece for the table as your guests sit down.

SERVES 6

2 (425 g/15 oz) cans tomatoes
10 ml/2 tsp tomato purée
1 garlic clove, crushed
grated rind and juice of ½ lemon
1 bay leaf
25 g/1 oz granulated sugar
5 ml/1 tsp Worcestershire sauce
salt and pepper
150 ml/¼ pint white wine
25 g/1 oz gelatine
450 g/1 lb frozen peeled cooked prawns, thawed
1 (425g/15oz) jar mussels, drained
10 cherry tomatoes, quartered
½ cucumber, chopped
vinaigrette dressing

GARNISH

chopped parsley
sliced cucumber

Heat the tomatoes (juice and all), tomato purée, lemon rind and juice, garlic, bay leaf, sugar and Worcestershire sauce in a saucepan with salt and pepper to taste and simmer gently for 5 minutes.

Put the wine in a small saucepan and sprinkle the gelatine on to the liquid. Leave for 3 minutes to swell, then heat gently until it has dissolved completely. Then add to the tomato mixture.

Purée in a food processor, blender or mouli-grinder until smooth. Pour into a 1.1-litre/2-pint ring mould and leave until set (3–4 hours).

Prepare the seafood salad by mixing the prawns, mussels, tomato and cucumber together and dressing it generously with vinaigrette.

When the tomato chartreuse is set, dip the mould carefully and briefly in warm water and turn out on to a serving platter. Spoon the seafood mixture into the centre, sprinkle with chopped parsley and surround the outside of the mould with slices of cucumber.

ESCALOPE OF TURKEY WITH NORWEGIAN GOAT'S CHEESE

The Norwegian goat's cheese adds a distinctive flavour, richness and a body to this dish. Small jacket potatoes with soured cream might go well with this.

SERVES 6

25 g/1 oz margarine

6 (175 g/6 oz) turkey escalopes

300 ml/½ pint chicken stock

150 ml/¼ pint white wine

75 g/3 oz Norwegian curd goat's cheese, grated

salt and pepper

GARNISH

225 g/8 oz grapes

225 g/8 oz button mushrooms

red wine

Melt the margarine in a large frying pan and then sauté the turkey escalopes on both sides. When sealed add the chicken stock and white wine, then simmer for 5 minutes.

Remove the turkey from the liquid and keep warm. Boil the liquid rapidly to reduce it and whisk in the goat's cheese. Keep whisking while the goat's cheese melts and the sauce thickens. Add salt and pepper to taste.

Pour the sauce over the turkey. Garnish with grapes and button mushrooms.

PINEAPPLE AND COINTREAU ICE CREAM

A tantalizing ice cream which is effortless to make and looks superb served in the scooped-out shells of a whole pineapple.

SERVES 6

1 pineapple

300 ml/10 fl oz double cream

150 g/5 oz icing sugar

45 ml/3 tbsp Cointreau

zest of 1 orange

Cut the pineapple lengthways right through including the top. Scoop out the flesh from both sides discarding the core. Be very careful not to damage the two empty shells.

Reserve a quarter of the pineapple flesh and chop it into small pieces to decorate the ice cream. Purée the remaining pineapple flesh in a food processor.

Whip the double cream and icing sugar to a stiff folding consistency. Stir in the Cointreau and pineapple purée. Pour the mixture into the two pineapple shells and freeze for at least 3 hours.

When ready to serve dot the pieces of pineapple flesh on top of the ice cream and sprinkle with orange zest.

WHAT THE EYE DOES NOT SEE

Potted Prawns with Fresh Herbs

Mexican Chicken

Rudyard Tart
with Lemon Custard

Nobody's heart is going to grieve over the production of this little meal but I think you will be pleased and surprised by your results.

POTTED PRAWNS WITH FRESH HERBS

A simple recipe for potting any shellfish but I suggest good quality prawns because brown shrimps seem so difficult to find.

SERVES 6

450 g/1 lb frozen peeled cooked prawns, thawed

oil for cooking

small bunch fresh basil leaves, chopped

chopped parsley

175 g/6 oz butter

1 garlic clove, crushed

pepper

GARNISH

thinly sliced tomato

thinly sliced cucumber

lemon twist

Drain the prawns carefully. Heat a heavy-bottomed saucepan with a little oil, and toss the prawns for about 1 minute while their water content evaporates. Scatter the chopped basil and parsley on top. Drain the prawns again, then transfer to individual ramekins.

Melt the butter in a clean pan with the crushed garlic and plenty of pepper. Pour the butter over the prawns to cover completely. Chill for 3–4 hours until set.

Arrange rings of tomato and cucumber slices on individual plates.

Turn out the moulded prawns by dipping each ramekin in hot water for a few seconds and then loosening the edges with a knife. Place the prawns in the centre of the tomato and cucumber slices and garnish with a twist of lemon. Serve with warm granary rolls.

MEXICAN CHICKEN

**A spicy colourful chicken casserole which makes its own sauce while cooking.
To accompany I recommend boiled new potatoes and broccoli florets.**

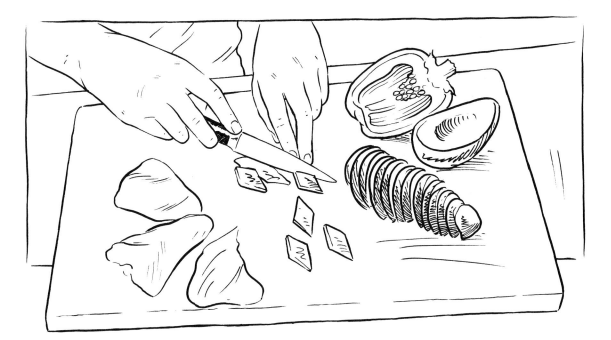

SERVES 6

4 (225 g/8 oz) chicken breasts
150 ml/¼ pint dry sherry
450 ml/¾ pint water
15 ml/1 tbsp thin honey
2.5 ml/½ tsp Tabasco
1 chicken stock cube, crumbled
2 firm avocados
1 red pepper, cored and seeds removed
cayenne pepper
20 ml/4 tsp arrowroot

Set the oven at 200°C/400°F/gas 6.

Cut the chicken breasts into three chunks and arrange in a single layer in an ovenproof dish. Mix the sherry, water, honey, Tabasco and stock cube together and pour over the chicken. Cover the dish and cook for 15 minutes.

Meanwhile, peel and slice the avocados. Cut the red pepper into diamond shapes about 2 cm/¾ inch long.

Remove the dish from the oven and scatter over the avocado slices and red pepper diamonds. Sprinkle with cayenne and return to the oven for another 5 minutes.

Transfer the chicken, avocado and peppers to a serving dish. Pour the liquid into a saucepan and bring to the boil. Mix the arrowroot with a little cold water and stir into the hot liquid to thicken it. Pour this sauce over the chicken and serve.

RUDYARD TART WITH LEMON CUSTARD

I'm not sure that Rudyard Kipling actually invented this dish but it is a deceptive adaptation of his namesake's irresistible treacle tart.

SERVES 6

2 (18cm/7 inch) shop-bought treacle tarts

10 ml/2 tsp bottled lemon juice

15 g/½ oz butter

300 ml/½ pint carton ready-made custard

150 ml/5 fl oz natural yogurt

grated rind and juice of 1 lemon

Set the oven at 180°C/350°F/gas 4.

Using a 5-cm/2-inch pastry cutter, cut six small rounds out of the tarts discarding the edges. Place these mini-tarts on a baking sheet and sprinkle with a little bottled lemon juice. Put a small knob of butter on each and bake for about 10 minutes.

Mix together the custard, yogurt, lemon juice and rind. Serve the tarts on a pool of the lemon custard.

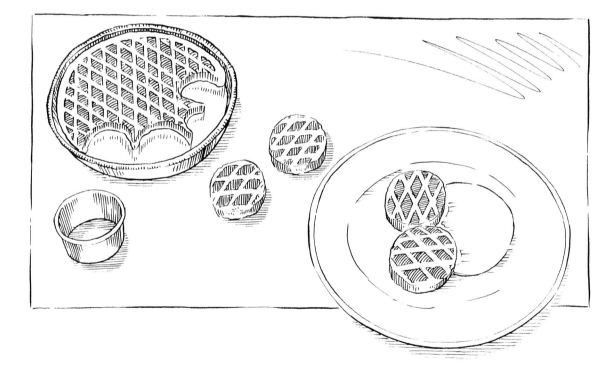

FROM THE RIVERS AND FORESTS

Woodland Salad

Rainbow Trout with Apricot and Pine Kernels

Blackberry and Apple Cobbler

There can be a degree of artistic licence in whether you actually gather produce in the forest or catch your own fish. Nonetheless this menu has a lovely natural feel to it and is full of ingredients which could have been found in the wild.

WOODLAND SALAD

Whole, baked black mushrooms filled with wood pigeon, nuts and fried bread, sitting on a bed of lettuce and watercress. Everything can be prepared in advance with the stuffed mushrooms ready to pop into the oven just before serving.

SERVES 6

6 (10-cm/4-inch) black flat mushrooms
30 ml/2 tbsp redcurrant jelly
45 ml/3 tbsp corn or groundnut oil
45 ml/3 tbsp walnut oil
3 slices of stale bread, cubed or crumbled
75 g/3 oz cashew nuts, crushed
3 wood pigeon breasts
1 garlic clove, crushed
15 ml/1 tbsp red wine vinegar
salt and pepper
1 oak leaf lettuce
1 bunch watercress

Clean the mushrooms and cut the stalks off. Arrange them open-side up on an oiled baking sheet and put a generous teaspoonful of redcurrant jelly on each.

Heat the two oils in a frying pan, then fry the bread and cashew nuts to a light golden colour. Remove and drain on absorbent kitchen paper.

Cut the wood pigeon in neat slices and add these to the pan. Stir in the crushed garlic and vinegar with salt and pepper to taste. Cook gently for a few minutes, then spoon the wood pigeon (including the oil and juices) into th mushrooms. Top with the fried bread and nuts. Set aside until just before serving.

Set the oven at 200°C/400°F/gas 6.

Arrange the oakleaf lettuce leaves on individual plates and put sprigs of watercress between them.

Bake the mushrooms for 5–10 minutes and then place one on each plate. Pour any extra juices on top.

TROUT WITH APRICOT AND PINE KERNELS

The trout can be cooked in advance and then reheated in the oven with no ill effects. I recommend you bake some sliced potatoes in milk and beaten egg to accompany this and perhaps also serve baked tomatoes.

SERVES 6

50 g/2 oz margarine	100 g/4 oz ready-to-eat dried apricots, sliced
plain flour	50 g/2 oz pine kernels
salt and pepper	100 ml/3½ fl oz sherry
6 rainbow trout	fresh chervil leaves, to garnish

Melt the margarine in a large frying pan. Mix a little flour with salt and pepper and use to coat the fish lightly. Shallow-fry the trout on both sides to a golden brown. Remove the fish from the pan and arrange them in an ovenproof dish.

Put the apricots and pine kernels in the pan and fry these for 2 minutes. Add the sherry and as it sizzles, pour the mixture over the fish. Set aside to reheat later.

Set the oven at 200°C/400°/gas 6.

When ready to serve put the dish in the oven for about 5 minutes (until good and hot). Either serve directly from the ovenproof dish or transfer to a platter and pour the juices over. Garnish with fresh chervil leaves (parsley will do if these cannot be found).

BLACKBERRY AND APPLE COBBLER

Instead of the labour of making pastry, this pie uses a top layer of miniature biscuits which make an attractive cobbled finish.

SERVES 6

25 g/1 oz butter
1.4 kg/3 lb apples, cored, peeled and sliced
2.5 ml/½ tsp ground cinnamon
2.5 ml/½ tsp ground nutmeg
100 g/4 oz soft light brown sugar
225 g/8 oz blackberries, fresh or frozen
350 g/12 oz Mini Hobknobs or similar children's biscuits

Melt the butter in a saucepan. Add the apples, spices and half the sugar. Cook gently for about 10 minutes. When the apples are tender, add the blackberries and transfer the mixture to a flameproof pie dish.

'Cobble' the top of the fruit mixture with the biscuits and sprinkle the remaining sugar on top. Place under a hot grill until the sugar is lightly caramelized. Serve with whipped cream.

ORIENTAL DECEPTION

Sesame Prawn Toasts

Chicken Satay
Fried Seaweed
Crispy Wonton with Plum Sauce

Spicy Duck Pancakes

Watermelon Lily with Exotic Fruits

If you can be bothered to get that rusty wok out and actually clean it, the rest is quite easy. A trip to the Chinese supermarket and if you want to go the whole way get out the chopsticks, jasmine tea and silk dressing-gowns! If your time and inclination permit, I recommend you make some little oriental decorations to garnish the dishes in this menu.

SESAME PRAWN TOASTS

Delicious fried toasts of prawns and sesame seeds which can be prepared in advance and then reheated.

SERVES 6

225 g/8 oz frozen peeled cooked prawns, thawed

10 ml/2 tsp soy sauce

1.25 ml/¼ tsp MSG

salt and pepper

1 egg

4 slices of white bread

75 g/3 oz sesame seeds

corn oil for frying

Put the prawns, soy sauce and MSG with salt and pepper to taste in a food processor and blend for 30 seconds. Add the egg and blend again.

Spread this mixture on the slices of bread and then cover the top with sesame seeds. You may find it easiest to put the sesame seeds on a plate and press the spread-side of the bread down on to them.

Heat about 2.5 cm/1 inch of oil in a wok. Fry the bread one slice at a time, cooking the spread-side first for about 1 minute and then the other side for about 30 seconds. Drain the toasts on absorbent kitchen paper. Set aside until just before serving.

Set the oven at 200°C/400°F/gas 6.

Reheat the toasts in the oven, then cut the crusts off and cut each slice into eight little oblongs or triangles.

CHICKEN SATAY

The real benefit of this combination is that, like the Sesame Prawn Toasts, it can be prepared in advance and cooked when required.

SERVES 6

45 ml/3 tbsp peanut butter

150 ml/5 fl oz natural yogurt

2 garlic cloves, crushed

10 ml/2 tsp soy sauce

salt and pepper and if you have them, ground coriander seeds

2 (175 g/6 oz) chicken breasts

Make the satay sauce by mixing together the peanut butter, yogurt, garlic and soy sauce with salt and pepper to taste.

Prepare the chicken by cutting each breast lengthways into six long strips. Thread the chicken on to 12 satay sticks in a zig zag. Coat the chicken strips all over with satay sauce and lay on a baking sheet. Set aside until required.

Set the oven at 200°C/400°F/gas 6.

Cook the chicken satay for 15 minutes. Serve the remaining satay sauce in a dish.

FRIED SEAWEED

The success of this dish depends on using very hot oil without setting your kitchen on fire! Be warned.

SERVES 6

450 g/1 lb spring greens

50 g/2 oz almonds, chopped

oil for frying

1 garlic clove, crushed

1.25 ml/¼ tsp MSG

caster sugar

salt

Prepare the greens by cutting out the stems, holding them tightly together and slicing them crossways into the finest 'shavings' you can manage. Lay them on a tray covered with absorbent kitchen paper and put them in an airing cupboard or other warm place to dry thoroughly for about 1 hour.

Heat 4 cm/1½ inches of oil, with the garlic in a wok and fry the almonds quickly until golden brown. Pour through a sieve and set the almonds aside.

Reheat the oil until it is smoky hot, remove from the heat for a few moments and then plunge all the shredded greens in and stir. (Do not be put off by all the sizzling.) Return the wok to the heat and cook for about 2 minutes. Drain off the 'seaweed' and place on absorbent kitchen paper to absorb any extra oil.

Transfer to a hot serving dish and sprinkle with the fried almonds and MSG with sugar and salt to taste. Serve immediately.

Anchovy Artichoke, Leek and Raisin Vinaigrette, Mangetout Salad

Pickled Pears

Woodland Salad, Blackberry and Apple Cobbler

Prepared Exotic Fruits

Asparagus Bouquet with Smoked Salmon

Oriental Deception: Sesame Prawn Toasts, Fried Seaweed, Chicken Satay, Crispy Wonton,
Spicy Duck Pancakes, Watermelon Lily with Exotic Fruits

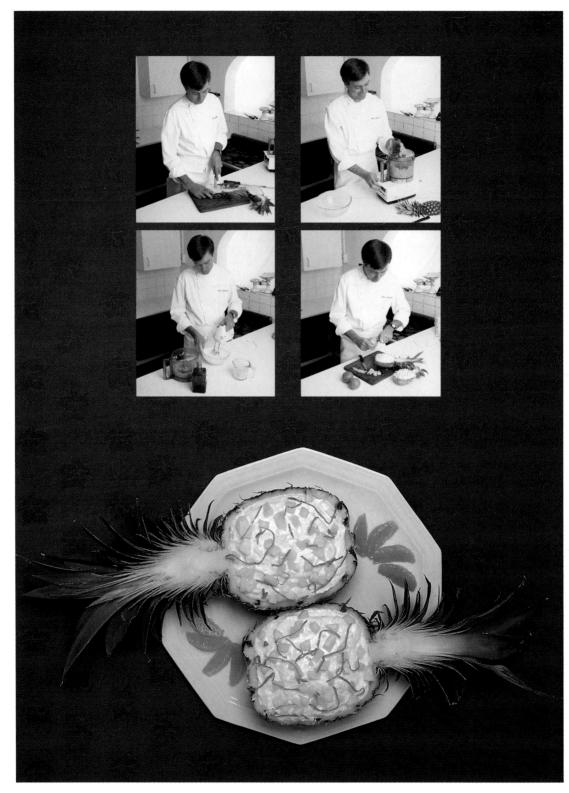

Pineapple and Cointreau Ice Cream

CRISPY WONTONS WITH PLUM SAUCE

Ready filled wontons are available from any Chinese or Oriental supermarket.
They are cheap so buy the most expensive available. The plum sauce is also
available in bottles but don't tell your guests all this.

SERVES 6

oil for frying

1 garlic clove, crushed

fresh root ginger, grated

2 packets stuffed wontons

1 bottle plum sauce

Heat about 2 cm/¾ inch of oil with the garlic and ginger. Fry the wontons until golden brown. Scoop them out and drain on absorbent kitchen paper. Put a small dish of plum sauce in the centre of your serving dish and scatter the fried wontons around it. Serve immediately.

SPICY DUCK PANCAKES

This shortcut version of famous crispy duck is unlikely to fool the Chinese but makes a very enjoyable imitation.

SERVES 6

1 packet Chinese pancakes
2 × 300 g/12 oz duck breasts
salt and pepper
soy sauce
1 bunch spring onions
½ cucumber
Hoisin sauce
oil for frying
1 garlic clove, crushed

Prepare the pancakes by laying them on a baking sheet in single layers between sheets of greaseproof paper. Spread a damp teatowel over the top. Place them in a very low oven or warming drawer to warm through.

Cut the duck, skin and all, into thin slices, then season well with salt, pepper and soy sauce. Prepare the spring onions and cucumber by slicing them lengthways into 7.5-cm/3-inch strips. Arrange these with a bowl of Hoisin sauce on a serving dish.

Heat 2 cm/¾ inch of oil with the crushed garlic in the wok. Fry the duck in the hot oil for 2–3 minutes. Scoop out and dry on absorbent kitchen paper. Arrange on a serving platter. The warm pancakes should be served stacked in a bamboo steamer or serving dish.

The guests themselves spread Hoisin sauce on the pancakes, fill them with shredded duck, onion and cucumber, roll them up and then tuck in.

WATERMELON LILY WITH EXOTIC FRUITS

A lovely presentation for a fresh fruit salad which will end your Oriental deception on a classic note.

SERVES 6

1 watermelon
2 bananas, sliced
2 oranges, peeled and segmented
1 (225 g/8 oz) can lychees, drained and halved
1 kiwi fruit, peeled, halved and sliced
2 passion fruit, halved and flesh scooped out

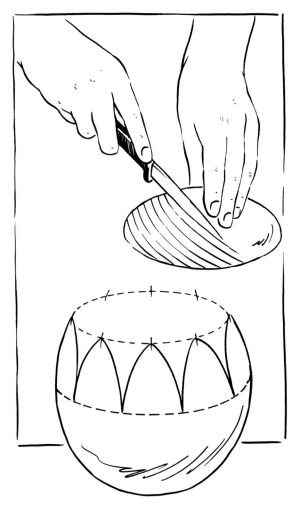

Hold the watermelon upright and if necessary trim a little off the bottom to make sure it sits straight. Cut off the top third and cut this into moon-shaped slices. Scoop the flesh out of the remaining watermelon with a large metal spoon and cube it for the fruit salad – you can discard some of the seeds but don't worry to pick them all out.

Mark the empty watermelon skin halfway down around its circumference. Then mark the top edge at eight evenly spaced points. From these points make curved V-shaped cuts down to the circumference line to form eight lily petals.

Mix the watermelon, banana, orange and lychees together. Fill the watermelon shell with these, then scatter the sliced kiwi and passion fruit on the top. Arrange the reserved slices of watermelon around the base of the lily.

ENTERTAINING ROYALTY

Smoked Salmon Blinis à la Russe

Fillet of Beef Béarnaise

Iced Grand Marnier Soufflé

Entertaining royalty – or your most deserving friends if the royals cannot make it. Although this menu uses some expensive ingredients, I am sure you will think it worth it.

SMOKED SALMON BLINIS A LA RUSSE

A slightly sweet pancake covered with soured cream and dill, topped with smoked salmon and Danish 'caviar' – it tastes as good as it sounds and the packet Scotch pancakes are quite undetectable.

SERVES 6

150 ml/5 fl oz soured cream

chopped fresh dill

freshly ground black pepper

6 Scotch pancakes

350 g/12 oz smoked salmon

lemon juice

GARNISH

red Danish lumpfish

black Danish lumpfish

Season the soured cream generously with chopped dill and freshly ground black pepper. Place the pancakes on individual plates and spoon a generous portion of soured cream on to each.

Carefully lay slices of smoked salmon right across each pancake, completely hiding the pancake and the soured cream.

Sprinkle the salmon with lemon juice and garnish with teaspoonfuls of red and black lumpfish right on the top.

FILLET OF BEEF BEARNAISE

As long as you are brave enough to serve this rare, it will be a sensational
dish and only needs very simple crisp vegetables to accompany it. This is the
easiest of joints to carve in the dining-room and I recommend you present it
whole on a line of radicchio leaves with a sprig of lamb's tongue lettuce nestling
on each leaf.

SERVES 6

1 (900 g/2 lb) fillet of beef

lard

GARNISH

1 radicchio

1 lamb's tongue lettuce

Set the oven at 220°C/425°F/gas 7.

Heat a little lard in a roasting tin on the
hob. Put in the fillet and literally scorch
the meat, sealing it on all sides. Then
transfer the tin to the oven and roast,
uncovered, for just 15 minutes. The meat
can rest for 10 minutes and the juices
should then be added to the béarnaise.

SAUCE BEARNAISE

90 ml/6 tbsp white wine vinegar

8 egg yolks

10 ml/2 tsp Dijon mustard

salt and pepper

225 g/8 oz unsalted butter

*10 ml/2 tsp mixed chopped fresh chives, tarragon
and parsley*

Boil the vinegar down by two-thirds to
make 30 ml/2 tbsp.

Put the egg yolks and mustard with salt
and pepper to taste in a food processor
and blend for 1 minute.

Melt the butter in a small saucepan and
bring to the boil. Add the reduced
vinegar to the butter and pour the boiling
liquid through the top of the food
processor with the blades running.
Within a few seconds the mixture will
thicken. Add the chopped herbs and
transfer to a sauce boat.

ICED GRAND MARNIER SOUFFLE

Although this recipe requires a little care, it is a most stylish pudding and is well worth the trouble.

SERVES 6

3 eggs, separated
150 g/5 oz caster sugar
grated rind and juice of 1 orange
juice of 1 lemon
45 ml/3 tbsp Grand Marnier
150 ml/5 fl oz double cream
cocoa, to decorate

Prepare six individual ramekins by sticking 2.5-cm/1-inch wide sellotape around the tops, so that 1 cm/½ inch stands above the rims.

In a large mixing bowl beat half the sugar and the egg yolks with an electric whisk until pale. Heat the orange rind and juice, lemon juice and Grand Marnier in a saucepan and pour on to the egg mixture while beating. Continue to beat until thick.

In separate bowls first whip the double cream until it is a folding consistency. Then (clean whisk, please) beat the egg whites until firm. Continue to beat the egg whites, while gradually adding the remaining sugar. (What a lot of beating! You should now have a bowl of the egg yolk mixture, a bowl of whipped cream and a bowl of whisked egg whites and sugar.)

Fold the cream into the egg yolk mixture and then carefully fold in the whites, using a metal spoon and the minimum of stirring.

Spoon the mixture into the ramekins right up to the top of the sellotape. Put in the freezer for 2 hours.

When ready to serve, remove the sellotape carefully and sprinkle the tops of the soufflés with cocoa. The soufflés will look as though they have miraculously risen in the ramekins.

BUFFET ENTERTAINING

While you should strive to make all food look attractive, the need for instant 'eye appeal' is most vital in a cold buffet. Over the centuries chefs have spent painstaking hours carving ice or lard statues, delicately applying aspic and turning or fluting vegetables to make the most elaborate of garnishes. To my mind this is quite unnecessary. If your buffet is full of exciting colours and includes some delectable dishes, it will automatically be visually appealing. The cheat's attitude to a buffet is once again to make life easy. Alas, it will not do just to buy cold meat and coleslaw from the deli but on the other hand too much hard slog and you will go off doing the buffet altogether. I have tried to suggest dishes which meet these criteria but only require the minimum of actual cooking.

You can obviously use these recipes for lunch or evening entertaining of any sort and the given quantities are suitable for 6 people for a normal meal. To help you calculate how much food you will need for a buffet for 12 people, I recommend the following combination as a guideline:

1 meat dish (recipe × 1 or 1½)
1 fish or vegetarian savoury dish (recipe × 1)
potato, rice or pasta salad (1 bowl)
2 other salad-type dishes
1 gooey pudding
1 fruit pudding
cheeses

WHOLE POACHED SALMON

You are not going to believe this recipe works but perhaps if I tell you that my catering kitchen cooks hundreds of salmon by this method every year, you will risk trying it. I use no fish kettles, no 'court bouillons' – the fish is simply cooked in the kitchen sink!

SERVES 6

1 (2.25 kg/5 lb) salmon

GARNISH

sliced cucumber

fresh fruit and vegetables

Clean the salmon thoroughly. Then arrange it upright in a S-shape in the bottom of a spotlessly clean sink. Make sure the plug is in.

Boil sufficient water to fill the sink (you will need to use a kettle and several large pans). Pour the boiling water around (not over) the fish until it is completely covered. Lay a sheet of foil across the sink to avoid losing the steam.

After 30 minutes remove the foil and simply pull the plug out to drain the water. Carefully lift the salmon out wearing rubber gloves and leave it to cool on a large flat dish.

When the salmon is completely cold, split the skin along the back and gently peel the skin and brown layer away – you will find the flesh is firm, deliciously moist and completely undamaged by cooking.

Transfer the salmon to a serving dish and garnish with vegetables and fruit. Have a look at the photograph on page 117.

CHICKEN WITH LEMON AND ALMONDS

This simple tangy cold chicken dish can all be prepared the day before, kept in the refrigerator and just assembled on the day.

SERVES 6

1 (1.8 kg/4 lb) chicken cooked (see method)

25 g/1 oz butter

25 g/1 oz plain flour

300 ml/¹/₂ pint chicken stock (see method)

grated rind and juice of 1 lemon

10 ml/2 tsp soy sauce

300 ml/10 fl oz single cream

salt and pepper

GARNISH

50 g/2 oz flaked almonds, browned under the grill

lemon slices

watercress

Boil the chicken with carrot, onion, celery, bay leaf and peppercorns for 45 minutes. Remove the flesh from the chicken, discard the skin and make some stock by returning the bones to the cooking liquid and boiling it up for 1 hour. Cut the chicken meat into neat strips and arrange on a serving dish. Cover and keep in the refrigerator until required.

Melt the butter in a saucepan. Stir in the flour and cook for 1 minute. Add the chicken stock (water and a dissolved stock cube will do if you have bought your chicken ready-cooked) and stir until smooth. Remove from the heat and add the lemon, soy sauce and cream with salt and pepper to taste. Allow to cool completely before putting in the refrigerator until needed.

Just before serving, coat the chicken with the sauce and sprinkle the browned almonds over it. Garnish with lemon slices and watercress.

HOMEMADE HONEY BAKED HAM

I would not dream of suggesting that you go to all the bother of buying green gammon and then boiling it and roasting it for hours. Instead you buy a normal 'easy-carve' ready-to-eat joint and transform it to taste and look homemade.

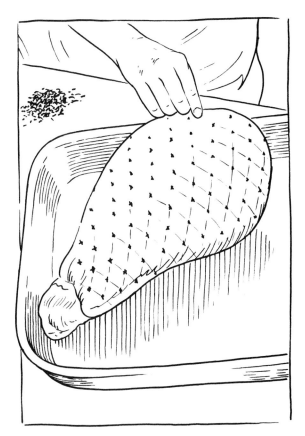

SERVES 6

1 cooked ham joint

cloves

45 ml/3 tbsp thin honey

15 ml/1 tbsp soft light brown sugar

grated rind and juice of 1 orange

30 ml/2 tbsp soft breadcrumbs

150 ml/¼ pint dry cider

Set the oven at 190°C/375°F/gas 5.

Score the ham with a series of crisscross cuts. Stud each cross with a clove, pressing it well into the meat. Put the joint in a roasting tin and spoon the honey evenly over it. Sprinkle on the sugar, the orange rind and finally the breadcrumbs.

Pour the orange juice and cider into the roasting tin and bake for 45 minutes. Once or twice during the cooking time take the tin out of the oven and spoon the liquid over the meat to baste it.

Garnish with orange slices and if liked, serve with Cumberland Sauce (page 47).

TUNA FISH KOULIBIACA

**A mixture of mushrooms, tuna and egg in a puff pastry parcel. This unusual
Eastern European dish is both a good filler and a delicacy.**

SERVES 6

oil for greasing

25 g/1 oz butter

2 onions, chopped

225 g/8 oz mushrooms, diced

1 garlic clove, crushed

1 (425 g/15 oz) can tuna fish

3 hard-boiled eggs, chopped

chopped parsley

salt and pepper

350 g/12 oz frozen puff pastry, thawed

egg wash

GARNISH

flowering chives

frisée lettuce

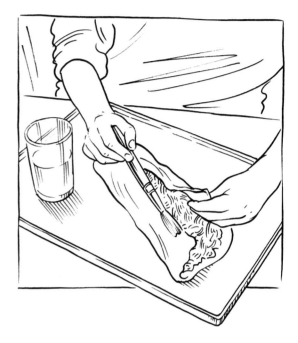

Oil a baking sheet. Set the oven at 200°C/
400°F/gas 6.

Melt the butter in a saucepan and fry
the onions until soft. Add the mushrooms
and garlic and cook for 2 minutes, then
drain well.

Flake the tuna into a bowl, stir in the
mushroom mixture and hard-boiled eggs
with parsley, salt and pepper to taste.

Roll out the puff pastry and trim it to a
30 × 20-cm/12 × 8-inch rectangle. Spoon
the fish filling down the middle and fold
over the two sides. Brush the pastry with
water where it overlaps and at each end
in order to make it stick. Roll the cylinder
over so the join is underneath, then fold
each end under neatly.

Garnish the top of the pastry with leaf
shapes cut from the pastry trimmings.
Brush with egg wash and transfer to the
prepared baking sheet. Bake for 25
minutes.

When cold cut a few slices and arrange
on a wooden board. If possible, garnish
with flowering chives and frisée lettuce.
Serve with Sauce Béarnaise (page 86).

TURKEY WITH PINEAPPLE AND TARRAGON CREAM

Cold turkey with fresh pineapple in a delicious tarragon cream sauce. This sauce can be equally effective with chicken or fish and is ideal for dressing up leftover cold food.

SERVES 6

450 g/1 lb cooked turkey, cut into small strips

1 egg

40 g/1½ oz caster sugar

45 ml/3 tbsp tarragon vinegar

salt and pepper

150 ml/5 fl oz double cream

½ fresh pineapple

GARNISH

paprika

chopped parsley

Arrange the cooked turkey meat on a platter.

Beat the egg and sugar in a bowl over a saucepan of simmering water until thick.

Put the tarragon vinegar in another pan, bring to the boil and add to the thickened egg. Add salt and pepper to taste. Leave to cool.

Lightly whip the cream and fold it into the egg mixture. Coat the turkey with the sauce.

Peel, core and slice the pineapple into small pieces and dot these on the sauce. Sprinkle lines of paprika and parsley on top.

COLD ROAST BEEF WITH PICKLED PEARS

Adding pickled pears to plain roast beef converts a rather dull traditional buffet item into something much more special.

SERVES 6

1 (1.8 kg/4 lb) joint topside or sirloin

3 Conference pears

175 ml/6 fl oz white wine vinegar

125 ml/4 fl oz water

100 g/4 oz soft light brown sugar

12 cloves

½ cinnamon stick

15 g/½ oz root ginger, peeled and sliced

grated rind of 1 lemon

GARNISH

seedless black grapes

radishes

Set the oven at 220°C/425°F/gas 7.

Roast the beef for 1 hour. Leave to cool completely before carving into thin slices.

Peel the pears and slice them crossways into round discs of varying sizes. (Don't throw the peel away.)

Heat all the pickling ingredients in a saucepan, then add the pear slices. Poach them gently for 5–10 minutes until soft. Scoop the pears out and set aside. Add the pear peel to the pan and cook until the liquid reduces by half.

Sieve the liquid and pour it over the pears. The pickle will now happily keep for 3 weeks or longer in an airtight jar so you may like to make a larger quantity.

Arrange the sliced beef on a serving platter, place the pears on top and spoon some of the pear syrup over. Garnish with black grapes and radishes.

LEEK AND RAISIN VINAIGRETTE

A very simple but effective dish to add something bohemian to your buffet selection.

SERVES 6

12 young leeks

75 g/3 oz raisins

150 ml/¼ pint white wine

150 ml/¼ pint olive oil

30 ml/2 tbsp white wine vinegar

75 g/3 oz soft light brown sugar

salt and pepper

chopped parsley

Peel the outer layer off the leeks and trim the green end. Blanch in boiling water for 2 minutes, then drain and chill under the cold tap.

Arrange the leeks in a shallow dish and scatter the raisins on top.

Heat the wine, oil, vinegar and sugar with salt and pepper to taste in a saucepan until the sugar is completely dissolved. Pour over the leeks and sprinkle parsley on top. Leave for at least 2 hours to cool and marinate.

CUCUMBER AND MINT MOUSSE

This refreshing dish would work well alongside chicken or fish on a buffet.

SERVES 6

oil for greasing

½ cucumber

225 g/8 oz cream cheese

150 ml/¼ pint mayonnaise

2.5 ml/½ tsp salt

5 ml/1 tsp caster sugar

5 ml/1 tsp Worcestershire sauce

10 ml/2 tsp lemon juice

10 ml/2 tsp gelatine

30 ml/2 tbsp water

150 ml/5 fl oz double cream

small bunch of fresh mint, chopped

GARNISH

1 bunch watercress

sliced cucumber

Oil a 1.1-litre/2-pint ring mould.

Peel the cucumber and remove the seeds. Then grate it into a sieve, reserving the juice.

Mix the cream cheese, mayonnaise, salt, sugar, Worcestershire sauce, lemon juice and grated cucumber together, preferably with an electric hand whisk, until smooth.

Put the reserved cucumber juice and the water in a small saucepan and sprinkle the gelatine on to the liquid. Leave to swell for 3 minutes, then heat gently until it has dissolved completely.

Add the gelatine mixture to the other ingredients and mix thoroughly. Lightly whip the double cream and fold into the mixture. Finally, stir in the chopped mint. Pour the mixture into the prepared ring mould. Chill for 3–4 hours until set.

To turn out, carefully ease the mousse from the sides of the mould with the tip of a knife and turn it on to a serving plate. Garnish with watercress in the centre and sliced cucumber around the edge.

Anchovy Artichokes

This recipe combines the attractive appearance of a fresh globe artichoke with the convenience of ready-prepared canned artichoke hearts, stuffed with a subtle anchovy pâté.

SERVES 6

1 large globe artichoke, trimmed

2 (175 g/6 oz) cans artichoke hearts, drained

PATE

225 g/8 oz cream cheese

60 ml/4 tbsp milk

1 small onion, grated and juice extracted

1 (75 g/3 oz) can anchovies, drained and chopped

2.5 ml/½ tsp Worcestershire sauce

pepper

chopped parsley

4 tomatoes, sliced

1 beetroot, finely diced

Cook the fresh artichoke by boiling it in salted water for 30 minutes. Leave to cool. Then pull out the inner leaves (carefully leaving the fleshy leaves intact) and with a metal spoon scrape off the hairy 'choke' in the middle. You will see the smooth heart underneath it.

Choose a suitable round serving platter and invert a saucer in the centre to make a raised platform. Place the globe artichoke on top of the saucer and arrange the artichoke hearts in a circle around it.

To make the pâté, blend the cream cheese, milk, onion juice (not pulp) and anchovies together into a smooth paste. Add the Worcestershire sauce with pepper and chopped parsley to taste.

Spoon some pâté into each artichoke heart and put the remainder into the centre of the globe artichoke. Sprinkle diced beetroot over each heart and garnish the platter with half slices of tomato. Your guests can help themselves to a whole stuffed heart or can dip leaves of the globe artichoke in the pâté.

AVOCADOS WITH BARBECUE SAUCE

Most people love avocados and peeled quarters with a spicy topping are a
favourite buffet item that I have served many times.

SERVES 6

4 rindless bacon rashers

3 ripe but firm avocados

lemon juice

1 round lettuce

1 radicchio

BARBECUE SAUCE

45 ml/3 tbsp mayonnaise

5 ml/1 tsp soy sauce

5 ml/1 tsp Worcestershire sauce

10 ml/2 tsp thin honey

5 ml/1 tsp Dijon mustard

salt

caster sugar

cayenne pepper

Cook the bacon until it is really crisp,
then drain it on absorbent kitchen paper.
When it is cold, chop it up.

Quarter and peel the avocados and
brush with a little lemon juice. Arrange
the avocado quarters on a bed of alternating lettuce and radicchio leaves.

Mix all the ingredients of the sauce
together with plenty of salt, sugar and
cayenne. Spoon a generous dollop of
the sauce on each avocado quarter and
sprinkle the chopped bacon on top.

BUFFET SALADS

You can be as creative as you like in making salads for a buffet. Not too many fussy, mixed ingredients but unusual combinations, strong contrasting colours and bold presentations will all work well. Here are some different salad ideas to get you underway:

NEW POTATOES WITH DILL MAYONNAISE

Wash some potatoes thoroughly (allow 100 g/4 oz per person), then simmer in boiling water until cooked. Drain and leave to cool. Mix some mayonnaise with chopped dill, add salt and pepper to taste and dilute with a little milk if necessary. Coat the potatoes in the dill mayonnaise.

WILD RICE SALAD

In a large pan of boiling water cook some wild rice (only a very little is needed) with some brown rice for 10 minutes, then add some white. When all the rice is tender, drain it and rinse under the cold tap. Add some finely diced red and green peppers and some canned sweetcorn. Dress with vinaigrette.

SAFFRON RICE SALAD WITH PRAWNS AND SLICED MANGETOUT

Put some long-grain rice (about 25 g/1 oz per person) in a pan of water with 15 ml/1 tbsp turmeric (saffron is obviously nicer but it is fearfully expensive). Bring to the boil and simmer for 15 minutes. Drain and rinse under the tap. Slice some mangetout into little strips and blanch them in boiling water for 30 seconds. Mix the mangetout and rice with some peeled cooked prawns and a dressing, then transfer to a serving dish.

RED CABBAGE SALAD WITH APRICOT AND CASHEW NUTS

Core and shred a red cabbage. Heat a little oil in a wok or pan, then toss the cabbage in it. Add some sliced dried apricots, cashew nuts, red wine vinegar, sugar, salt and pepper. Transfer to a serving dish and sprinkle with chopped parsley.

BUFFET SALADS

MIXED LEAF SALAD

Choose a variety of fresh lettuces or leaves such as endive, radicchio, oakleaf, lamb's tongue or Little Gem. Separate the leaves (only wash them if it is really necessary), then arrange them in layers around a bowl or plate. Dress with lemon juice and olive oil.

TOMATO AND APPLE VINAIGRETTE

Slice tomatoes and dice a crisp green apple finely. Arrange the tomato slices on a flat dish, sprinkling the apple between each layer. Dress with vinaigrette.

PASTA AND BASIL SALAD

Cook some pasta twirls (allow 25 g/1 oz per person) according to the instructions on the packet, then rinse well under cold water. Chop and fry some bacon and mushrooms. Add equal quantities of pesto (bottled basil dressing) and olive oil with salt and pepper to taste and toss the pasta in it. Add the mushrooms and bacon, then dot a few fresh basil leaves on top.

SPINACH AND CROUTON SALAD

Prepare the croûtons by dicing stale bread and lightly frying in oil with a little garlic. Choose small tender spinach leaves, cut the stems out and shred coarsely. Dress the spinach before scattering the croûtons on top. Watercress, orange or bacon all make good additions to this salad.

MANGETOUT AND ORANGE SALAD

Prepare and blanch some mangetout (about 50 g/2 oz per person). Peel some oranges and carefully segment them without any pith. Mix the two ingredients casually on a serving dish and dress with oil, white wine vinegar, salt and pepper.

BEETROOT, APPLE AND WALNUT SALAD WITH SOURED CREAM

Slice some cooked beetroot into a serving bowl. Sprinkle some chopped walnuts and diced apple on top. Add salt and pepper to taste or some dried chives to some soured cream and spoon this liberally over the top.

BUFFET SALADS

WARM VEGETABLE SALAD

Blanch some broccoli and cauliflower florets, julienne carrots, baby sweetcorn and strips of red pepper in boiling water until tender but still firm. Drain and rinse them under cold running water. Heat some sunflower oil in a wok or large frying pan with some crushed garlic, salt and pepper to taste. Add the vegetables with a little white wine. Stir-fry the vegetables for just 1 minute. Transfer to a dish and serve.

ASPARAGUS WITH CHOPPED EGG AND SPRING ONION VINAIGRETTE

A good tip for cooking fresh asparagus without damaging it is to use a flat roasting tin instead of a saucepan. Lay the asparagus in a tin and cover with water. Bring to the boil, then simmer gently for 8 minutes. Drain carefully (a wine rack is ideal to help you to do this), then leave to cool. Chop up some soft-boiled eggs and mix with sliced spring onions, tarragon vinegar, oil, salt and pepper. Coat the asparagus tips with the dressing.

AVOCADO, TOMATO, MOZZARELLA AND BLACK OLIVE SALAD

Peel, halve and slice some avocados. Cut some Mozzarella cheese and beef tomatoes in slices. Arrange these three ingredients in parallel lines across a serving dish. Scatter with halved black olives and dress with olive oil, lemon juice and pepper.

JULIENNE OF CUCUMBER AND TOMATO WITH YOGURT DRESSING

Cut even strips of cucumber and tomato (discarding the seeds), mix together gently and arrange in a serving dish. Add salt, pepper and chopped parsley to some natural yogurt and spoon this into the centre of the salad.

WATERCRESS, ORANGE AND GOAT'S CHEESE SALAD

Mix some watercress with fresh orange segments and flaked goat's cheese. Dress with oil, wine vinegar and salt.

CHOCOLATE AND CHESTNUT TERRINE WITH PLUM COULIS

An Italian-style layered terrine of chestnut, chocolate and biscuits – very rich but balanced well by the plum coulis I have suggested as an accompaniment.

SERVES 6

50 g/2 oz butter
40 g/1 1/2 oz caster sugar
225 g/8 oz plain chocolate
175 g/6 oz chestnut purée
150 g/5 oz macaroon biscuits
100 g/4 oz Nice biscuits
45-60 ml/3–4 tbsp cream sherry

PLUM COULIS

1 (425 g/15 oz) can red plums
10 ml/2 tsp lemon juice
10 ml/2 tsp caster sugar

Line a 450 g/1 lb loaf tin with oiled greaseproof paper.

Beat the butter and sugar together until smooth. Melt the chocolate in a bowl over a pan of simmering water. Crush the macaroons by covering them with a tea-towel and hitting with a rolling pin. Mix the butter and sugar, melted chocolate, macaroons and chestnut purée together.

Spread one-third of the mixture into the prepared loaf tin, smoothing it out evenly. Arrange a single layer of Nice biscuits in the tin and spoon some sherry over the biscuits to soak them completely. Add another layer of the mixture, then the remaining biscuits and sherry and a top layer of the mixture. Chill for 3–4 hours until the terrine has set hard.

Lift the terrine out of the tin by holding the edges of the greaseproof paper. Unwrap it carefully and cut it in cross-ways slices. Arrange on a serving dish.

To make the plum coulis, remove the stones from the plums and add the lemon juice and sugar. Purée in a blender. Serve the coulis in a small bowl alongside the terrine.

BANANA AND LIME MOUSSE

A light easy mousse which is set with a packet jelly.

SERVES 6

1 (75 g/3 oz) packet lime jelly
300 ml/1/2 pint hot water
grated rind and juice of 1 lime
300 ml/1/2 pint evaporated milk, chilled
150 ml/5 fl oz double cream
3 fresh bananas, sliced
1 fresh lime slice, to decorate

Dissolve the jelly in the hot water. Add the lime rind and juice and leave to cool.

Whip the evaporated milk until it doubles in volume and thickens. (It must be chilled to whip.) Whip the double cream until it is thick.

When the jelly is beginning to set, fold the milk and cream into it. Then add the sliced bananas. Transfer the mixture into a soufflé dish and, when set, decorate the top with the lime slice.

CARAMELIZED ORANGES AND PINEAPPLE

These two acidic fruits, sweetened with caramel, complement one another
beautifully both in colour and flavour.

SERVES 6

6 oranges
1 small fresh pineapple
225 g/8 oz caster sugar
300 ml/½ pint water

Carefully take strips of zest off the orange skins with a zester (page 14). Then peel and slice the oranges. Hold the slices together by skewering the oranges with wooden cocktail sticks.

Cut the pineapple into six long sections, peel and core them, slice crossways and again hold each section of slices together with a wooden cocktail stick.

Arrange the oranges and pineapple randomly in glass dish and sprinkle the orange zest on top.

Prepare the caramel by heating the sugar and water together in a heavy-bottomed saucepan over a low heat. Do not stir; allow the sugar first to dissolve and then slowly turn to a bubbling golden brown. Pour the boiling caramel over the fruits and it will set hard.

If you make the dessert in advance, the caramel will begin to dissolve after a few hours making it easer to serve.

CHEAT'S HOMEMADE AUTUMN TRIFLE

Trifle is one of those marvellous puddings which never goes out of fashion – the trouble is that it has so many different elements and is therefore rather time-consuming to make. My version uses fresh fruit to make it look homemade but everything else comes out of a packet.

SERVES 6

450 g/1 lb fresh dark plums

1 (225 g/8 oz) packet trifle sponge

100 ml/3½ fl oz sherry

1 (400 g/14 oz) can blackberries, drained

450 ml/¾ pint carton custard

300 ml/10 fl oz double cream

100 g/4 oz blackberries, fresh or frozen, to decorate

Cut the plums crossways into 5-mm/ ¼-inch discs and ease each slice off the stone. Arrange the slices in lines up the side of a glass serving dish reserving a few for the top.

Cut the trifle sponges in half and trim them to fit into the bottom of the serving dish. Moisten with some sherry and then put half the canned blackberries in a layer over them. Cover with a layer of custard. Trim the remaining trifle sponges to make another complete layer. Moisten with the remaining sherry, add a layer of the remaining blackberries and top with the rest of the custard.

Whip the double cream to a soft but firm consistency. Pipe parallel lines of cream on to the top of the trifle and decorate the edge with cream rosettes. Finally arrange the fresh or frozen black-berries and reserved plum slices in neat stripes between the cream lines.

HAZELNUT MERINGUE WITH RASPBERRIES

An adaptable and quite delectable classic dessert that freezes well. If you have not experienced it, you have been missing out.

SERVES 6

oil for greasing

100 g/4 oz peeled hazelnuts

4 eggs whites

225 g/8 oz caster sugar

2.5 ml/¹/₂ tsp white wine vinegar

300 ml/10 fl oz double cream

1 (275 g/10 oz) can raspberries, drained

icing sugar

fresh raspberries, to decorate (optional)

them in the oven for 10 minutes, then chopping them up in a food processor.

Whisk the egg whites until stiff. Gradually add the sugar while continuing to beat until the whole mixture is very firm. Mix in the vinegar and chopped nuts.

Spoon the mixture evenly into the prepared tins and bake for 40 minutes. When cooked, turn the meringues on to a wire rack to cool.

Whip the double cream. Spoon a little into a piping bag to decorate the top and mix the remainder with the raspberries. Spoon this filling on to one meringue and cover with the other. Pipe rosettes of cream on top and dust with icing sugar. Decorate the cream rosettes with fresh raspberries, if used.

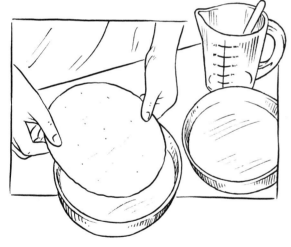

Lightly oil two 20-cm/8-inch sandwich tins and lay a disc of non-stick baking parchment on the bottom of each. Set the oven at 180°C/350°F/gas 4.

Prepare the hazelnuts by browning

PREPARED EXOTIC FRUITS

More a formula than a recipe for transforming fresh fruits into an extravagant and mouth-watering buffet centre-piece. Fruits of different shapes, sizes and colours are prepared in contrasting ways and then assembled in a loosely arranged pattern. Doesn't that sound artistic! You will need at least six varieties of fruit but the final selection will depend on the season and price – I have made some suggestions for you to consider.

LARGER FRUITS

Pineapple Quartered lengthways, including the spiky top. The flesh cut off the skin, sliced into triangles, then rearranged.

Ogen or Galia melon Cut into a basket shape, the flesh then cut with a baller, mixed with black grapes and piled back into the melon.

Honeydew or water melon Cut into long boats. The flesh cut off the skin but leaving one end attached.

Pawpaw Cut lengthways into thick oval-shaped slices retaining the attractive seeds in each centre.

MEDIUM FRUITS

Clementines The skin scored into six sections – carefully peeled from the top but left attached at the base like a lily.

Bananas, apples and pears These all need brushing with lemon juice to retain colour.

Apricots, plums, peaches and nectarines Halved or quartered and stones removed.

Grapes Left on the stalks but trimmed into miniature bunches. Two colours can be effectively intertwined.

Pomegranate Shell left on and the whole fruit cut into eight sections.

SMALL FRUITS

Passion fruit Halved.

Lychees and Cape gooseberries Scored into four sections and the skin peeled back like petals.

Figs or large strawberries Cut lengthways into quarters.

Small berries, cherries and currants of all sorts Kept whole .

Choose a large platter or tray and depending on its beauty, cover with leaves, ferns or a cloth. Place the biggest pieces of fruit on the platter first – not necessarily symmetrically but creating a clear pattern. Then arrange the medium ones in sections in between. Finally scatter the smallest berries or fruits over.

If you look at the photograph on page 78, you will soon get the idea.

ROASTS, VEGETABLES AND GRAVY

How we would all love a cheat's solution to that most demanding of British traditions, the Sunday roast. Alas, I have no perfect answer – packet joints, pre-prepared vegetables and ready-mix gravies are total anathema to me. However, the problems of producing tender roast meats which can be carved speedily, hot vegetables and tasty gravies still exist and perhaps these few suggestions will help you.

ROAST MEATS

Firstly, I suggest you choose a joint with the ease of carving as well as flavour in mind. If you are catering for four or six people, a leg, shoulder or rib roast is fine but if you are catering for eight or ten, I recommend you choose easier joints to carve such as rolled and boned loins or topsides.

Secondly, you should roast with a minimum of fat and start the joint off in a hot oven – even if you prefer slow cooking – and reduce the temperature after the first 30 minutes.

The old formula of 20 minutes to every 450 g/1 lb and 20 minutes over is fine if you are cooking an average size joint (about 1.8 kg/4 lb) of an even shape at a medium temperature. However, a 3.5-kg/8-lb joint of beef cannot possibly be roasted for 3 hours and remain edible. I prefer my lamb and beef pink while my pork and chicken should be well cooked but still moist. Each to his own of course and I will not venture further in dictating how long you should cook your meat. The only other tips I would offer are:

Resting the joint Leave time after cooking for the joint to rest before carving. This will help to firm up the meat, both making it easier to slice and retaining more juices. The joint should be removed from the oven and its fat before resting; it can either sit in a warming drawer or just be covered with foil and several tea-towels to keep it hot.

French roasting If you find your chicken or other fowl gets dry, try a French roast. Pour a mixture of water and wine into a roasting tin to a depth of about 2.5 cm/1 inch and add about 20 minutes to your normal cooking time. Do not cover the bird. You should get a very tender juicy result with a ready-made base for your gravy.

BOILED VEGETABLES

You may be disillusioned to hear that even in the finest of restaurants they don't time the cooking of vegetables so perfectly that your portion is just ready at the same moment as your main course – they actually pre-cook the vegetables and then reheat them. Why do we so often spoil a meal by either waiting for the leeks to cook while the rest of the food gets cold or cooking the broccoli so far in advance that what finally emerges is no longer recognizable?

The following chart gives suggested pre-cooking and reheating instructions for different vegetables. Blanching means the vegetables are plunged into boiling salted water to soften, drained and either plunged into iced water or held under the cold tap. This process ensures a good retention of nourishment and also preserves perfect colour. The reheating methods are very simple to follow and vary according to the dish you are making.

VEGETABLE	PRE-COOKING	REHEATING
Asparagus	Blanch for 8 minutes	Warm in a covered dish with butter in a low oven
Broccoli	Blanch for 3–5 minutes	Plunge back into boiling water
Brussels sprouts	Blanch for 5–8 minutes	Plunge back into boiling water
Cauliflower	Blanch for 5–8 minutes	Plunge back into boiling water
Carrots	Blanch for 7–8 minutes	Toss in hot margarine
Celery	Blanch for 3–5 mintues	Toss in a heated pan
Courgettes	Blanch for 2 minutes	Sauté in butter with fresh herbs
French beans	Blanch for 5–7 minutes	Toss in hot margarine
Leeks	Blanch for 3–5 minutes	Toss in a heated pan
Mangetout	Blanch for 30 seconds	Toss in hot margarine
Red cabbage	Boil until tender	Sauté with vinegar, apple and redcurrant jelly
Runner beans	Blanch for 5–7 minutes	Toss in hot margarine
Spinach	Blanch for 1 minute	Purée or chop – reheat in oven
Squashes	Boil until tender, then purée	Reheat in oven
Swedes	Boil until tender, then purée	Reheat in oven
Sweet peppers	Blanch for 1 minute	Sauté in oil
White cabbage	Boil until tender	Sauté in margarine with raisins

ROAST VEGETABLES

Oddly enough for a shortcutting, pre-cooking, time-saving cook like myself, I do not recommend par-boiling potatoes, parsnips or celeriac unless it is absolutely unavoidable. For crisp golden brown roast vegetables I suggest:

- ☐ The vegetables should be completely dried before putting into fat
- ☐ Use very hot, clean lard
- ☐ Turn vegetables after the first 10 minutes
- ☐ Cook near the top of a hot oven (200°–220°C/400–425°F/gas 6–7)

GRAVY

Gravy will make or break your roast meal and a last-minute scramble of stirring flour and water in the bottom of a roasting tin is something we can all do without. I suggest you make gravy in a saucepan well in advance and simply add the meat juices just before serving if you wish to do so.

My gravy always has a roux base (equal quantities of flour and margarine or dripping) to thicken the appropriate stock (home-made, carton or cube), water and some red or white wine. Then the fun begins and you can experiment with the addition of a whole host of other ingredients to enhance the flavour. Try some of these combinations:

For beef	Add horseradish, prepared mustard and pepper
For chicken	Add lemon juice and tarragon
For duck	Add orange rind, mixed herbs and brandy
For lamb	Add garlic, redcurrant and mint
For pork	Add honey, prepared mustard and apricot
For veal	Add brown sugar, wine vinegar, dry sherry and mixed spice

Finally, add just a little gravy browning to make your sauce golden or a little more for a deep rich brown. Alas, grey is a very unappetizing colour!

YORKSHIRE PUDDING

Why Yorkshire pudding worries some competent cooks I shall never understand. There is not even any need to cheat and I have included the recipe just to prove how simple it is to make good Yorkshire pud.

THE BATTER

lard or dripping

300 ml/½ pint milk

100 g/4 oz plain flour

1 egg

2.5 ml/½ tsp salt

Melt some lard or dripping in a roasting tin (or individual tins) to cover the bottom to a depth of 3 mm/⅛ inch. Put the tin in the oven until the fat is 'smoky' hot.

Put the milk, flour, egg and salt in a food processor and blend until completely smooth. Alternatively, whisk the ingredients together. If necessary, sieve the mixture to make sure every lump of flour has disappeared.

Pour the mixture into the prepared tin and bake on the top shelf of a hot oven (200°–220°C/400°–425°F/gas 6–7) for about 20 minutes.

SPECIAL
DINNERS
FOR TWO

Surely the most special occasion of all is a celebratory dinner with only one guest. True you may know him or her very well and he or she may be very forgiving when it comes to culinary skills. All the same, set out to do your best and your food should shine.

I have included some starters, main courses and desserts. It is by no means essential to serve three courses – two (or even one) good courses are preferable to several mediocre ones.

Quantities in this section are all for just two although they can easily be multiplied for larger gatherings. Some of the recipes are, however, a little more elaborate than those in the preceding chapters so take your time and practise à deux before serving at a banquet.

A great advantage I find when I cook dinner for two is that I can make lots of mess and then expect my guest to wash up and make the coffee!

MELANGE OF MARINATED SALMON AND SOLE

If this is your first venture into uncooked fish, keep faith and I think you will be pleasantly surprised. The marinating of fish does in fact change the texture and tenderizes it just as cooking does but without any loss of flavour. Ask your fishmonger to fillet and skin the fish.

SERVES 2

100 g/4 oz salmon fillet (from the tail)

100 g/4 oz lemon sole fillet

25 g/1 oz mangetout, trimmed and blanched (page 108)

1 orange, segmented

50 g/2 oz red grapes, halved and pips removed

MARINADE

grated rind and juice of 1 lime

45 ml/3 tbsp oil

15 ml/1 tbsp lemon vinegar

5 ml/1 tsp pink peppercorns

chopped fresh dill

salt

caster sugar

Prepare the marinade by mixing the ingredients together with chopped dill, salt and sugar to taste.

Cut the fish into pencil-thin strips about 7.5 cm/3 inches long. Put in a bowl and pour the marinade over the fish. Work the marinade in a little so the strips of fish are completely coated. Cover and leave for 3–4 hours.

When ready to serve, add the mangetout and fruits to the fish and mix gently. Arrange the mixture randomly on individual plates and spoon over the remaining marinade.

LEBANESE PRAWN SOUP

A delightful summery soup which takes only moments to make. I have described how to make it in a food processor but the same results can be achieved by hand – it will just take a little longer.

SERVES 2

175 g/6 oz frozen peeled cooked prawns, thawed

1/3 cucumber, peeled, seeds removed and roughly chopped

150 ml/1/4 pint water with 1/2 vegetable stock cube dissolved in it

300 ml/10 fl oz Greek thick yogurt

crushed garlic

salt and pepper

GARNISH

peeled cooked prawns

cucumber slices

Put the prawns in a food processor and chop for a few seconds (try not to pulp them). Transfer the chopped prawns to a large bowl.

Put the cucumber and stock in the food processor and blend until smooth. Add this mixture to the prawns. Fold in the yogurt and add garlic, salt and pepper to taste. Chill for 3–4 hours.

Serve chilled, garnished with prawns and cucumber slices.

Barbecue Party Fare

Scallops with Bacon and Waterchestnuts, Breast of Duck with Horseradish Mousse,
Melange of Marinated Salmon and Sole

Miniature Fish Stew

Selected buffet dishes: Whole Poached Salmon, Cucumber and Mint Mousse, Chicken with
Lemon and Almonds, Saffron Rice Salad with Prawns and Mayonnaise, Cold Roast Beef
with Pickled Pears, Cheeseboard, Hazelnut Meringue with Raspberries

Praline Fondue

Red Fruit Kissel with Lemon Sorbet

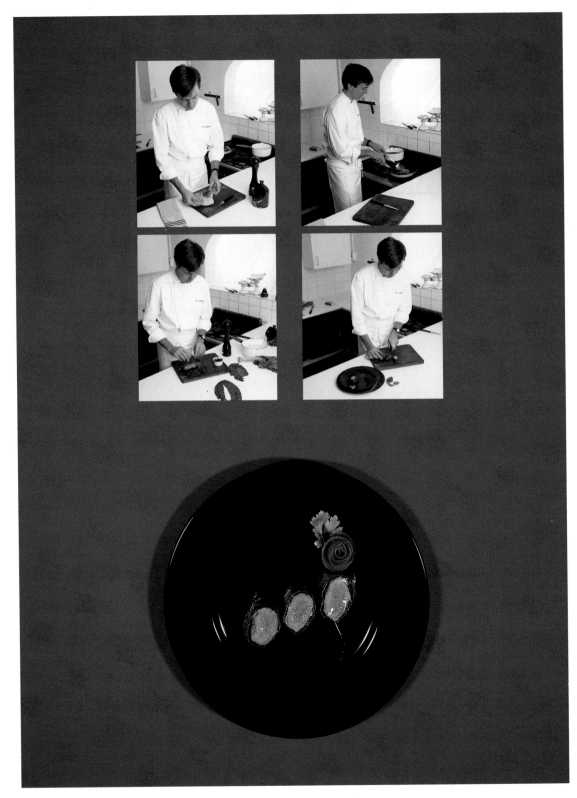

Fillet of Lamb Epinard

SOUFFLÉED ANCHOVIES ON TOAST

The mixture of anchovies, capers and fromage frais puffed up with egg whites and then lightly grilled, is irresistible. This dish takes no time to produce but must be prepared the moment before eating. Soaking the anchovies in milk reduces the saltiness and helps to separate them.

SERVES 2

4 canned anchovy fillets, soaked in a little milk

15 ml/1 tbsp capers

grated rind and juice of ½ small lemon

30 ml/2 tbsp fromage frais

10 ml/2 tsp grated Parmesan cheese

freshly ground black pepper

1 egg white

2 slices wholemeal bread

Set the grill to hot.

Chop the anchovies into small pieces and mix with the capers, lemon rind and juice, fromage frais and Parmesan cheese. Add freshly ground black pepper to taste.

Whisk the egg white in a dry bowl until stiff, then using a metal spoon, fold it into the anchovy mixture.

Cut the crusts off the bread and toast one side under a hot grill. Spoon the anchovy mixture on to the uncooked side of the bread and grill for 1 minute until golden brown. Serve immediately accompanied by a little tomato and spring onion salad.

BREAST OF DUCK WITH HORSERADISH MOUSSE

A very classy starter which if successfully executed will immediately label you as
a great chef and, more importantly, excuse you from producing a main course.
The duck is served thinly sliced and pink with a rich, spicy mousse to
complement it.

SERVES 2	MOUSSE
oil for cooking	40 g/1½ oz cream cheese
1 (225 g/8 oz) duck breast	30 ml/2 tbsp mayonnaise
50 g/2 oz fresh spinach (small young leaves)	10 ml/2 tsp horseradish sauce
walnut oil	dash of Worcestershire sauce
lemon juice	30 ml/2 tbsp water
salt and pepper	5 ml/1 tsp gelatine
sweet basil sprigs to garnish	30 ml/2 tbsp double cream

Oil two small ramekins. Set the oven at
200°C/400°F/gas 6.

Heat a little oil in a frying pan and seal
the duck breast on both sides, cooking the
skin to a crisp golden brown. Transfer
the duck to a roasting tin. Cook in the
oven for 5 minutes. Allow the duck to
cool.

Prepare the mousse by first blending
the cream cheese, mayonnaise and horseradish and Worcestershire sauces. Put the
water in a small saucepan and sprinkle
the gelatine on to the liquid. Leave for 3
minutes to swell and then heat gently
until it has dissolved completely. Stir into
the cream cheese mixture.

Lightly whip the double cream, fold
this into the mixture and add plenty of
salt and pepper. Put the mousse in the
prepared ramekins and chill for 3–4
hours until set.

Choose the two most elegant main
course plates you can find in the cupboard or borrow from a friend. Shred the
spinach leaves, dress them with oil, lemon
juice, salt and pepper and arrange in a
neat half-moon shape on each plate.
Turn the mousses out and place them in

the centre of the uncovered half of the
plates.

Carefully cut the duck breast into thin
slices and arrange these in a crescent
shape around the mousse, overlapping
on to the spinach, as shown in the
photograph on page 114. Finish with a
sprig of sweet basil next to each mousse.

ASPARAGUS BOUQUET

**An original presentation of two of the most delicious foods:
asparagus and smoked salmon.**

SERVES 2

12–16 asparagus spears, trimmed
75 g/3 oz smoked salmon
2 strips of red pepper
50 g/2 oz butter
2 spring onions, chopped
chopped parsley
chopped fresh tarragon
salt and pepper

Cook the asparagus in boiling salted water for 8–10 minutes. Drain and chill under the cold tap.

Lay the smoked salmon out and overlap or fold it to form two long bands about 4 cm/1½ inches wide. Use the smoked salmon to tie 6–8 sticks of asparagus together.

Put the tied bunches on individual plates and splay out the tops to resemble the shape of a bunch of flowers. Wrap a strip of red pepper over the smoked salmon to form a central band on each bouquet.

Melt the butter. Add the spring onion with herbs, salt and pepper to taste and pour this over the asparagus tips.

SCALLOPS WITH BACON AND WATERCHESTNUTS

A traditional way of serving scallops is to wrap them in bacon. The combination
is delicious but it seems a shame to hide the lovely appearance of the scallops.
This simple recipe uses small queen scallops in a classic sauce and served with
bacon rolls filled with crunchy waterchestnuts. If possible the mixture should
be served in two clean scallop shells (ask your fishmonger).

SERVES 2

3 rindless rashers streaky bacon

1 (100 g/4 oz) can waterchestnuts

100 ml/3½ fl oz white wine

chopped fresh marjoram

salt and pepper

10 queen scallops (or 4 large ones)

30 ml/2 tbsp double cream

1 egg yolk

Oil a baking sheet. Set the oven at 200°C/
400°F/gas 6.

Stretch out the bacon rashers, cut each one in two and wrap a whole water-chestnut up in each length. Put the bacon rolls on the prepared tin and cook in the oven for about 10 minutes.

Put the white wine in a shallow sauce-pan and boil it for 1 minute. Reduce the heat and add chopped marjoram, salt and pepper to taste. Then poach the scallops gently for 2 minutes. Remove the scallops from the liquid and stir in a mixture of the cream and egg yolk (called a liaison) which will thicken the sauce. Be careful not to allow the sauce to boil.

Arrange the scallops in the shells, pour the sauce over them and place three bacon rolls on each.

ESCALOPE OF VEAL WITH KUMQUAT AND CAPERS

Have you ever wondered what those lovely-looking miniature oranges are
actually good for? They have no juice and taste like uncooked marmalade. In
this dish, however, they add a unique tangy flavour to veal.

SERVES 2

50 g/2 oz butter

2 (175 g/6 oz) escalopes of veal, each cut into
2 pieces

salt and pepper

10 ml/2 tsp lemon vinegar (lemon juice will do)

25 g/1 oz kumquats, thinly sliced

20 ml/4 tsp capers, diced

chopped parsley, to garnish

Heat the butter in a frying pan, taking care not to brown it. Season the pieces of veal with salt and pepper and sauté for 2 minutes on each side.

Remove the veal from the pan on to individual hot plates. With the butter still bubbling vigorously add the lemon vinegar, kumquats and capers. Let this sizzle for 30 seconds, then pour the whole mixture over the veal and serve. Garnish with a little chopped parsley.

FILLET OF LAMB EPINARD

I obviously like dishes containing spinach (it must be a childhood Popeye complex) because here is another one. In this dish the lamb is served very pink and moist with a wrapping of spinach leaves – it therefore should not need a sauce, just some crisp spring vegetables.

SERVES 2

1 (450 g/1 lb) boned loin or best end of lamb
50 g/2 oz spinach leaves
15 ml/1 tbsp redcurrant jelly
½ garlic clove, crushed
salt and pepper
2 firm tomatoes, to garnish

Set the oven at 180°C/350°F/gas 4.

Remove the lean meat from the fat in a single piece. Heat a frying pan with the lamb fat in it until the pan is well greased. Remove the fat and cook the fillet of lamb in the pan until it is sealed all over. Cover the pan and continue to cook for a further 5 minutes. Remove the meat on to absorbent kitchen paper to drain.

Blanch the spinach leaves in boiling water for 30 seconds, then drain and chill. Unravel the leaves and place them overlapping to form a square ready to wrap the lamb. Spread the spinach with the redcurrant jelly and garlic with salt and pepper to taste. Place the lamb in the centre and wrap it up like a parcel. Transfer to an oiled baking sheet, cover with foil and put in the oven for 10 minutes or until hot.

Serve by slicing the lamb crossways into 2.5-cm/1-inch thick slices. Garnish with tomato roses, made by peeling each whole tomato in a continuous strip (eat the tomato!) and then rolling the peel up like a reel of sticky tape.

ENTRECOTE DIJONNAISE

Quite my favourite way to eat a steak – topped with Dijon mustard, onion and brown sugar. I recommend a small dish of potatoes cooked in stock and a green salad as accompaniments.

SERVES 2

1 onion, chopped
25 g/1 oz butter
15 ml/1 tbsp Dijon mustard
1 egg yolk
salt and pepper
2 (175 g/6 oz) entrecôte steaks
15 ml/1 tbsp demerara sugar

Set the grill at high.

Fry the onion in the butter until it is golden brown. Drain and turn on to absorbent paper to dry out. Mix the onion with the mustard and egg yolk. Add plenty of salt and pepper.

Seal the steaks under the hot grill on one side. Remove from the grill and press the onion mixture in a thick layer on to the uncooked side. Sprinkle the sugar over the top and replace under the grill until the sugar is almost burning. Serve immediately.

If you prefer your steak well cooked, grill both sides before topping with the onion mixture.

WOOD PIGEON WITH FRESH CRANBERRIES

A lovely winter or even Christmas dish best served with miniature jacket potatoes and green vegetables.

SERVES 2

15 g/½ oz margarine
30 ml/2 tbsp oil
4 wood pigeon breasts
100 g/4 oz fresh cranberries
25 g/1 oz caster sugar
grated rind and juice of 1 orange
ground cinnamon
mixed spice
100 ml/3½ fl oz port
salt and pepper

Heat the oil and margarine together in a frying pan. Gently sauté the pigeon breasts for 5 minutes on each side. Remove on to absorbent kitchen paper and keep warm.

Put the cranberries, sugar, orange rind and juice, and spices in a saucepan and simmer for about 5 minutes. The cranberries will soften, create their own juice and pop open when ready. Add the port, and add salt, pepper and sugar to taste.

Spoon the cranberry mixture on to individual plates. Halve or slice the wood pigeon breasts and arrange on top of the cranberry mixture.

MINIATURE FISH STEW

The joy of this dish is that there is only one thing to put into and take out of the oven. The preparation can be done well in advance. Make sure your fishmonger descales and carefully fillets the fish. You may need to smile very sweetly because you only want very small quantities.

SERVES 2

1 (175 g/6 oz) seabass or bream fillet

1 (275 g/10 oz) red mullet, filleted but not skinned

2 baby carrots

1 celery stick

1 small courgette

100 ml/3½ fl oz white wine

150 ml/¼ pint water with ½ fish stock cube dissolved in it

5 ml/1 tsp chopped fresh dill

5 ml/1 tsp chopped fresh coriander

Set the oven at 180°C/350°F/gas 4.

Cut the fish into neat pieces and arrange these skin-side up in two oven-proof gratin dishes.

Prepare the vegetables and cut them into 4-cm/1½-inch lengths. Blanch the carrots and celery in boiling water, then drain and chill.

Arrange the vegetables including courgettes between the pieces of fish, round-side up. Pour the wine and stock over the fish. Sprinkle the dill on the seabass and the coriander on the mullet. Bake for 15 minutes and serve.

ROAST POUSSIN WITH LEMON AND PEPPERCORNS

This sophisticated-looking dish is surprisingly easy to produce.

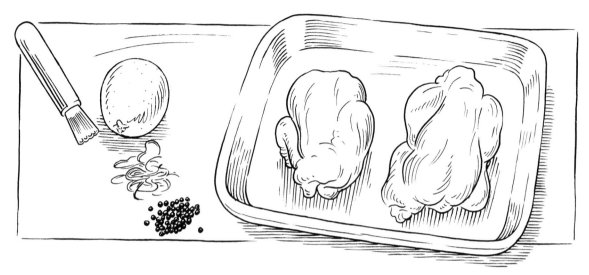

SERVES 2

2 poussins

melted butter or margarine

1 lemon

150 ml/¼ pint water

½ chicken stock cube, crumbled

125 ml/4 fl oz dry sherry

10 ml/2 tsp green peppercorns

5 ml/1 tsp pink peppercorns

10 ml/2 tsp arrowroot mixed with a little cold water

watercress, to garnish

Set the oven at 200°C/400°F/gas 6.

Put the two poussins in a small roasting tin and brush them with melted butter or margarine.

Take the rind off the lemon in little strips with a zester and then squeeze the lemon juice. Mix the lemon juice (not the rind) with the water, stock cube, sherry and two types of peppercorns and pour the mixture around the poussins. Roast, uncovered, for 40 minutes.

When cooked, pour off the liquid into a small saucepan, bring to the boil and stir in the arrowroot to thicken.

Put the poussins on individual plates, pop a little tuft of watercress in their bottoms and pour the sauce and peppercorns in a complete circle around them. Finally scatter the strips of lemon rind on to the sauce and serve.

CRÈME BRÛLÉE

Crème Brûlée is one of those mythical dishes which conjures up hours of painstaking beating over a saucepan of boiling water and a great deal of skill. My version, which has been universally admired, is just mixed together, then baked in the oven and finally popped under the grill. Make four ramekins – two for tonight and two for tomorrow – you will enjoy it so much!

SERVES 2 (twice!)

butter for greasing

4 egg yolks

75 g/3 oz caster sugar

4 drops of vanilla essence

300 ml/10 fl oz single cream

50 g/2 oz demerara sugar

Butter four ramekins. Set the oven at 150°C/300°F/gas 3.

Put the egg yolks, caster sugar and vanilla essence in a bowl and mix well. Heat the cream in a saucepan until just before it boils up, then pour over the egg yolk mixture, stirring while you do so.

Pour the mixture into the prepared ramekins and stand them in a roasting tin. Pour cold water into the tin around the ramekins to a depth of 2.5 cm/1 inch. Bake for 40 minutes. Then remove from the tin and allow to cool.

Set the grill at hot.

Divide the demerara sugar equally between each ramekin, spreading it out evenly. Place under the grill until they are well browned. Allow to cool again before serving.

RED FRUIT KISSEL WITH LEMON SORBET

Kissel is an eastern European dish of puréed red berries thickened with arrowroot. With the addition of a scoop of sorbet the dish is irresistible.

SERVES 2

450 g/1 lb mixed berries (strawberries, raspberries, blackcurrants, redcurrants, blueberries or blackberries)

15–45 ml/1–3 tbsp caster sugar

15 ml/1 tbsp arrowroot mixed with water

1 (100 g/4 oz) carton lemon sorbet

Set one-third of the fruits aside and put the remainder in a food processor, blender or mouli-grinder. Make a smooth purée, adding some water if necessary.

Heat the purée and the sugar in a saucepan until boiling and then stir in the arrowroot mixture. Transfer the thickened purée to a dish and add the remaining fruit. Currants and blueberries should be added whole while strawberries and blackberries need cutting into small pieces.

Chill the kissel for 3–4 hours. When ready to serve ladle it into soup bowls and put a round scoop of sorbet in the centre of each one.

CHOCOLATE-DIPPED FRUITS

One of the most stylish and tantalizing desserts I know. Individual fresh fruits half-coated in dark or white chocolate and then just devoured.

SERVES 2

oil for greasing

100 g/4 oz plain chocolate

100 g/4 oz white chocolate

ANY THREE OF THE FOLLOWING FRESH FRUITS:

apricots (quartered)
black or green grapes (whole)
cherries (whole)
kiwi fruit (skinned and cut in eighths)
peaches or nectarines (sliced)
seedless grapes (in pairs)
strawberries (whole)

Oil a baking sheet.

Choose ripe but firm fruits of contrasting colour – allow 3 of each per person.

Break the two types of chocolate into small pieces and put in separate bowls over saucepans of simmering water. Stir the chocolate occasionally and allow to melt without getting too hot.

Hold each fruit or piece of fruit individually and half-dip it in either the plain or white chocolate. Put on the prepared baking sheet to set.

Arrange the fruits in lines on a serving dish and refrigerate until ready to serve.

CREPES SUZETTE

If you are busy, lazy or both, I recommend you buy the pancakes rather than make them yourself. In any event the pancakes can be prepared in advance and have nothing to do with the creation of your Suzette.

SERVES 2

50 g/2 oz butter

2 galette pancakes

20 ml/4 tsp caster sugar

grated rind and juice of 1 small orange

30 ml/2 tbsp brandy

1 small orange, peeled and sliced, to decorate

Melt the butter in a frying pan. Brush each pancake with some of the butter, sprinkle with caster sugar and fold into a triangle. Put the folded pancakes back into the pan and fry for a few moments until very hot.

Add the orange rind and juice to the pan. When this is boiling, add the brandy and 'flambé'. (To do this, either tilt your pan towards the gas flame and let it catch or simply put a match to it.)

When the flames die down, transfer the pancakes and juices to hot plates and decorate with orange slices.

Serve immediately.

DRAMBUIE ZABAGLIONE

This warm seductive dessert must be made and then eaten immediately. If you beat the mixture too much, it will separate or if you leave it to stand, it will spoil. As with so many things – timing is everything!

SERVES 2

2 egg yolks

50 g/2 oz caster sugar

45 ml/3 tbsp Drambuie

ground nutmeg

Mix the egg yolks, sugar and Drambuie together in a bowl and set it over a saucepan of simmering hot water. Beat the mixture constantly while it warms gently. It will become frothy and quite thick.

Transfer to martini-type glasses, dust with a little nutmeg and serve.

PRALINE FONDUE

Fondues are always associated in my mind with intimacy and laughter. In the Alps there is a tradition that if you drop bread off your fondue fork, you must kiss the lady next to you at the table. This unusual dessert fondue can continue the tradition as well as being very special to eat. The accompaniments can be as varied as you like such as ring doughnuts, cut into small discs, cubes of cake, marshmallows or small pieces of fresh fruits arranged on a platter.

SERVES 2

50 g/2 oz almonds
100 g/4 oz caster sugar
300 ml/10 fl oz double cream
5 ml/1 tsp vanilla essence
15 ml/1 tbsp cornflour
100 ml/3½ fl oz sherry

Oil a small baking sheet.

It is surprisingly easy to make your own praline. Put the almonds and 50 g/2 oz of the sugar in a small saucepan and set over a low heat. When the sugar has melted, stir the mixture and then continue to cook until it is a dark nutty brown. Turn out of the pan on to the prepared tin. Leave to cool and set. When it is hard, break the praline into pieces and chop or process into a coarse powder.

To make the fondue, heat the cream, remaining sugar and the vanilla in a fondue pot, taking care it does not boil. Mix the cornflour and sherry together and stir this in to thicken the cream. Then, add the praline.

Transfer the pot on to a fondue burner set in the middle of the dining-table. With long forks your guest and you skewer the accompaning cubes of cake or pieces of fruit and dip them into the hot praline.

SUCCESS WITH BARBECUES

I am sure that you must have shared the dubious pleasure of a barbecue party where the man of the house becomes chef for the day. Invariably you are served with blackened lumps of meat (origin unknown), which somehow manage to remain raw and cold inside. I fully support the new era tradition of a non-cooking husband taking responsibility for the barbecue, but his ability to light the garden bonfire does not necessarily qualify him to cook. I think a little advice and some gentle cheating will do him no harm at all.

Firstly, you need a good generous fire in the barbecue. Charcoal meanness is the most common failing. Secondly, you must let the fire really get going before you start cooking. Unlike a cooker, the barbecue fire can easily be dampened down with a spray or splash of cold water but you cannot increase the heat on demand.

Thirdly, it is important to understand what the barbecue is trying to achieve. Obviously the ambience of cooking and eating outside is part of the attraction but in addition the food you cook is meant to be:

juicy through being sealed by the barbecue flame

flavoursome through the self-basting of fat dripping on to the charcoal, then steaming back on to the food

lightly smoked by the charcoal or wood itself

PRE-COOKING

At the risk of offending any purist charcoal grill chef I suggest you can achieve most of the desired results with a degree of pre-cooking in an oven to help things along. I am not recommending that you pre-cook steaks, chops or fish, but chicken, sausages or larger pieces of meat can definitely be helped by part-cooking and then finishing off on the barbecue to get the authentic flavour. I have given several recipes using pre-cooking in various ways. As a general rule if the meat is well wrapped in foil while it is in the oven, the outside will not colour. Your cheating will therefore remain our secret.

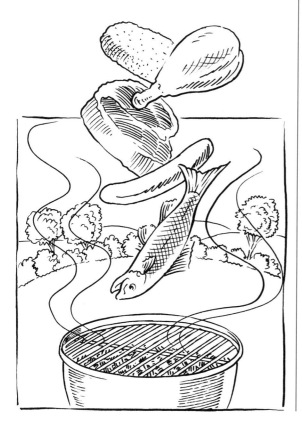

MARINATING

I have also included recipes using a marinade. The purpose of marinating barbecue food is either to add another flavour or to tenderize a cheaper cut of meat. The use of spices and herbs will season the food; oil will prevent the food losing its natural moisture; wine or lemon juice will break down tough fibres and a pinch of bicarbonate of soda is an ancient Chinese tenderizer – goodness knows what it does but it sounds good!

BARBECUED VEGETABLES

Mostly I find that barbecued vegetables sound better than the end results taste and salads are both easier and more attractive. If you are doing vegetables, however, I recommend the following:

☐ Potatoes and larger vegetables: Blanch beforehand or wrap in foil parcels.
☐ Smaller vegetables: Thread on kebab skewers for easy turning and brush with oil during cooking.

BARBECUED PARTY FARE

Three simple ideas for really tasty barbecue snacks with a difference.

SERVES 6
HUNGRY DEVILS ON HORSEBACK

6 large sausages

6 rindless bacon rashers

25 g/1 oz blanched almonds

175 g/6 oz dried prunes, stones removed

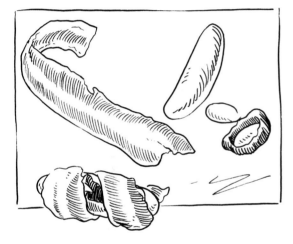

Set the oven at 180°C/350°F/gas 4.

Pre-cook the sausages in the oven for about 20 minutes.

Put an almond in the centre of each prune. Cut slits in the sides of the sausages and stuff three of the prunes into each. Wrap a bacon rasher round and round the sausages like a helter-skelter.

Barbecue until the bacon is crisp and the sausage is browned.

SERVES 6
CHICKEN LEGS WITH SWEET BASIL AND PARMESAN

6 chicken drumsticks

45 ml/3 tbsp natural yogurt

1 garlic clove, crushed

6 basil leaves, chopped

30 ml/2 tbsp grated Parmesan cheese

salt and pepper

Pre-cook the drumsticks by simmering in a pan of boiling water for 12 minutes.

Mix the yogurt, garlic, basil and Parmesan cheese into a paste. Add plenty of salt and pepper. Roll the drumsticks in the paste, then barbecue until golden brown.

SERVES 6
MARINATED SPARE-RIBS

12 spare-ribs

30 ml/2 tbsp tomato ketchup

15 ml/1 tbsp fruity sauce

15 ml/1 tbsp soy sauce

10 ml/2 tsp Worcestershire sauce

15 ml/1 tbsp thin honey

salt and pepper

Arrange the spare-ribs in an open dish or tray.

Mix all the sauces and honey together with salt and pepper to taste. Pour over the spare-ribs and leave to marinate for at least 2 hours.

Barbecue for 5–10 minutes on each side, basting occasionally with the marinade.

CHILLI PRAWNS

Prawns are quite excellent on the barbecue provided they are not overcooked.
Bear in mind that the pink prawns we buy have been pre-cooked.

SERVES 6

*18 frozen peeled cooked jumbo or Mediterranean
prawns, thawed*

MARINADE

15 ml/1 tbsp chilli sauce

2 drops of Tabasco

½ small onion, grated

15 ml/1 tbsp lemon juice

30 ml/2 tbsp tomato purée

30 ml/2 tbsp soft light brown sugar

15 ml/1 tbsp chopped parsley

Arrange the prawns in an open dish. Mix all the marinade ingredients together and coat the prawns in the mixture. Leave for at least 1 hour, then remove the prawns from the marinade and barbecue over a hot fire for 1 minute each side.

Serve on a bed of lettuce with a side dish of mayonnaise flavoured with lemon rind and juice.

LEG OF LAMB IN PEPPER CRUST

Definitely a dish which needs pre-roasting but as long as you don't give the
secret away, no one will ever know. The lamb with its delicious pepper crust only
requires traditional mint and redcurrant to go with it.

SERVES 6–8

1 (1.8–2.25 kg/4–5 lb) leg of lamb
30 ml/2 tbsp green peppercorns
30 ml/2 tbsp wholegrain mustard
15 ml/1 tbsp rock salt
15 ml/1 tbsp chopped fresh rosemary
1 garlic clove, crushed
oil

Set the oven at 200°C/400°F/gas 6.

Put the lamb on a wire rack in a roasting tin and cover completely in foil.

Roast in the oven for 1¼ hours. Remove the joint and allow to cool.

Prepare the crust by crushing the peppercorns and mixing with mustard, salt, rosemary and garlic.

Brush the joint with a little oil, then spread the pepper mixture on to it. Cook on the barbecue for about 45 minutes, turning frequently and dousing any flames with a water-spray.

Present the joint whole and carve at the table.

STUFFED CALAMARI

Young squid cooks very effectively on a barbecue and makes an unusual
summer dish. Squid will not keep well so it should be cooked at the last minute.

SERVES 6

6 whole cleaned squid (bodies about 13 cm/ 5 inches long)
2 courgettes, diced
1 yellow pepper, cored, seeds removed and diced
1 (400 g/14 oz) can tomatoes, drained
shredded fresh tarragon
75 g/3 oz Cheddar cheese, grated
salt and pepper
oil

Chop the tentacles of the squid into small pieces and cook them in boiling water for 2 minutes with the courgettes and peppers. Drain and combine this mixture with the tomatoes, tarragon and cheese. Add salt and pepper to taste.

Make sure the squid bodies are completely clean inside. Then fill them with the vegetable mixture. Brush with oil. Cook over a moderate fire for 5–10 minutes, turning frequently.

Marinated Teriyaki Steak

If you would like to add a little oriental touch to your barbecue this is the dish to do it.

SERVES 6

675 g/1½ lb rump steak, cut into 4-cm/1½-inch cubes

1 red pepper, cored and seeds removed

1 green pepper, cored and seeds removed

MARINADE

50 ml/2 fl oz dry sherry

60 ml/4 tbsp soy sauce

2 garlic cloves, crushed

15 g/½ oz root ginger, grated

30 ml/2 tbsp soft light brown sugar

15 ml/1 tbsp lemon vinegar

30 ml/2 tbsp oil

2.5 ml/½ tsp mixed spice

Put the steak in a bowl. Heat all the marinade ingredients together in a saucepan. Bring to the boil, then allow to cool. Pour the marinade over the steak and leave for 12 hours.

Cut the peppers into 2.5-cm/1-inch squares. Thread the pieces of beef and pepper alternately on six long wooden skewers. Cook on the hottest possible barbecue for less than 2 minutes. Serve immediately with the marinade offered in a separate bowl.

PORK TENDERLOIN WITH CELERY AND APRICOT SAUCE

Pork tenderloins are one of the best larger pieces of meat to cook over a fire without any cheating being necessary. They have the advantage of being lean and their small diameter means they can be properly cooked through.

SERVES 6

900 g/2 lb pork tenderloin

45 ml/3 tbsp Dijon mustard

salt and pepper

SAUCE

25 g/1 oz margarine

1 onion, chopped

1/2 head celery, chopped

50 g/2 oz ready-to-eat dried apricots, chopped

30 ml/2 tbsp cider vinegar

Spread the tenderloins with Dijon mustard and sprinkle with plenty of salt and pepper. Cook on the barbecue for 30–40 minutes, rolling over occasionally.

To make the sauce, melt the margarine in a small saucepan and cook the onion until soft. Add the celery, apricots and vinegar with salt and pepper to taste. Cook for a further 5 minutes.

Cut the meat into 1-cm/1/2-inch slices, reheat the sauce and serve alongside.

CHICKEN BREASTS WITH HAM AND RICOTTA

Another barbecue cheat but this time the meat is first sealed on the fire and then cooked through in the oven.

SERVES 6

6 chicken breasts
100 g/4 oz ham, minced
100 g/4 oz Ricotta cheese
grated rind and juice of 1 lemon
10 ml/2 tsp thin honey
15 ml/1 tbsp chopped parsley
salt and pepper
300 ml/½ pint boiling water with 1 chicken stock cube dissolved in it

GARNISH

1 lemon, cut in 6 wedges
1 bunch watercress

Set the oven at 200°C/400°F/gas 6.

Light the barbecue and as soon as the flames die down, cook the chicken breasts quickly on both sides, if possible giving them a scorched pattern from the grill. Once golden brown remove from the barbecue and return to the kitchen. (From here on the chicken is cooked in the oven so you may like to barbecue some vegetable kebabs so as not to waste the fire).

Cut a pocket slot in the side of each breast. Mix the ham, cheese, lemon rind and juice, honey and parsley together and add plenty of salt and pepper. Fill the chicken pockets with the ham mixture and put them in a roasting tin. Pour over the hot chicken stock.

Cook in the oven for 20 minutes. Remove the breasts from the tin and arrange them around the edge of the barbecue to keep warm.

Garnish with lemon wedges and watercress.

WHOLE BAKED TUNA FISH

As this is the last recipe in a whole book of short cuts and cheats, I thought I would end with a completely authentic dish of no practical value whatsoever. A whole fresh tuna is baked in its own skin over a fire pit of burning cedar logs. I prepared this dish for party of 100 people in France – the locals loved it!

SERVES 60!

1 (9–13.5 kg/20–30 lb) tuna fish, gutted and cleaned

Begin by digging a hole in the ground – about 120 × 45 × 30 cm/48 × 18 × 12 inches deep. Line bricks or stones along the two long edges to make a wall about 20 cm/8 inches high each side of the pit.

Light a large wood fire in the hole and let it burn fiercely until all the flames have died and you are left with hot smouldering logs.

Lay six metal rods across the two brick walls and rest the tuna fish on them. Turn the fish every 20 minutes. After a while the skin will go crisp and form a sealed cocoon. Continue to cook for 2–3 hours, testing occasionally by putting your fingers inside the fish's belly to see if it is hot right through. The fire may need stirring up or the odd new log added as long as it does not flame too much.

When the cooking is complete transfer the fish to a carving block, cut open the skin and reveal the sumptuous half-smoked, half-baked flesh inside.

DRINKING WITH STYLE

I have already said that putting a cheap wine into an expensive bottle is an unacceptable form of cheating, although with the amount of snobbery associated with wine these days, I am sometimes very tempted. There is the undisguised snob who flatly refuses to drink anything but only certain years of French château-bottled wine. Even worse there is the inverted snob who claims that all wines from non-wine producing third world countries will automatically be superb. There must be some middle ground somewhere between these two.

The good cheat selects wines from right across the globe and does not mind if his 'Burgundies' are Californian or his Cabernets are Bulgarian. He considers the occasion and his guests. If his wines are vibrant and sparkling then perhaps the party will be too. When the guests are traditional and well-aged, he can choose wines to match!

The next point to my mind is why does 'drinking' imply alcohol? We are all supposed to be diligent about not 'drinking' and driving but the only alternative on offer tends to be the inevitable mineral water – yawn yawn. Perhaps we should serve Passion Fruit Juice, Elderflower Champagne or Homemade Lemonade. I have given some simple recipes for these and other 'soft' drinks you may like to try.

My final gripe on Great British drinking relates to that innocent question, 'What would you like to drink?' In certain homes this means 'Do you want a gin and tonic?' In others there is a motley collection of duty-frees which is kept out of sight and the game is to guess available combinations. To drink with style I think you should offer one or two specific drinks or mixes. Your choices need not be expensive but should be celebratory and fun. I have listed some different ideas at the end of this chapter.

Choosing Wines

There is no such thing as the 'right' wine to go with a specific dish. Different wines do indeed suit different foods but, equally different wines suit different people. At the end of the day you should drink what you enjoy and what you can afford.

That said there is, however, a great deal of pleasure to be had from developing a taste in wine, experimenting with different types and discovering what to drink when. Don't be afraid to ask a wine merchant for advice and don't limit yourself to wines you have heard of – some of the lesser known offer the best value and individuality. I have listed below both traditional and some more unusual ideas for wines with food.

Canapés

Champagne; sparkling hock; Pinot Blanc.

Soups

Dry sherry; white Rioja; Gewürztraminer.

Salad Starters

Sancerre; Moselle; Californian Sauvignon; Orvieto; Bulgarian Chardonnay.

Seafood

Muscadet; New Zealand Sauvignon; German Riesling; Gewürztraminer.

White Fish

Chablis; Bergerac; Portuguese Dão; Tuscan whites; Pinot Grigio.

Oily Fish

Fine white burgundy, Puligny or Meursault; white Rioja; Australian or Californian Chardonnay.

White Meat

Beaujolais; Romanian Pinot Noir;
Fumé Blanc; Valpolicella;
Bulgarian Cabernet.

Red Meat

Clarets; Chilean, Argentinian,
Bulgarian or Hungarian Cabernet;
Californian Zinfandel.

Game

Red burgundy; Rioja;
Côtes du Rhone; Australian Shiraz;
South African Roodeberg.

Pasta Dishes

Chianti Classico; Côtes de Ventoux;
Montepulciano d'Abruzzo;
Californian Cabernet.

Cheese

Red burgundy; Beaujolais; Rhone;
port.

Desserts

French, Russian or Australian
Champagne;
New Zealand Late Harvest Reisling;
Australian Orange Muscat;
Monbazillac.

ALTERNATIVE SOFT DRINKS

Citrus Sparkle Thick slices of orange, lime and lemon in a tall glass filled up with sparkling water.

Elderflower Champagne To my mind this is the ultimate soft drink – it needs at least a week to get its fizz but is well worth the waiting. Put 3 heads of elderflower, the juice of 1 lemon, 450 g/1 lb granulated sugar and 30 ml/2 tbsp white wine vinegar, in a large saucepan with 4.5 litres/8 pints water. Bring to the boil, then leave for 24 hours. Strain and bottle.

Homemade Lemonade Halve and squeeze 3 lemons. Then pour 1.1 litres/ 2 pints of boiling water over the juice and lemon skins. Add 75 g/3 oz caster sugar and leave to stand for 30 minutes. Discard the lemon skins. Chill the liquid and serve with ice and sliced strawberries.

Iced Tea with Mint Make ordinary tea and leave to brew for 3 minutes. Strain into a glass jug and add caster sugar to taste. Fill up the jug with ice cubes, some lemon slices and whole mint leaves.

Passion Fruit Juice Now available in cartons but it needs diluting, with still or sparkling mineral water and decorating with other fresh fruits.

Crushed Blackberries Crush equal quantities of blackberries and caster sugar together, then add 3 parts of water and pour over crushed ice.

INVITING COMBINATIONS

Kir   Just 5 ml/1 tsp Crème de Cassis in a glass of very dry white wine.

Kir Royale   As above but replace the wine with champagne or sparkling wine.

Crème de Mure   More difficult to find but more subtle than the cassis, this blackberry syrup is also delicious with white wine.

Crème de Mure Spritzer   Blackberry syrup, white wine and fizzy water.

Bellini   Finely diced rather than puréed fresh ripe peaches, topped up with champagne or sparkling wine.

Bucks Fizz   Although very well known still the perfect Sunday morning drink – champagne or sparkling wine with freshly squeezed orange juice.

Champagne Framboise   Soak raspberries in brandy and add a spoonful to sparkling wine or champagne.

Pineapple and Cider Cup   Diced fresh pineapple soaked in brandy and mixed with equal parts of lemonade and dry cider.

Long Gin and IT-alian   Single measure of gin, double measure of dry Martini in a tall glass of ice and soda.

Pimms   Soak fresh mint, cucumber and orange in the Pimms mix and dilute liberally with lemonade and dry ginger. This drink is invariably served too strong and sweet.

Bishop's Hot Punch   Spices, orange and lemon zest, cream sherry and water all brewed up together.

Mulled Wine   1 glass brandy to 1 bottle cheap red wine with sugar, cloves, cinnamon and orange zest served piping hot.

THE
CHEAT'S
LAST RESORT

The questions I am asked most often as a professional chef are: do I ever have disasters and what would I do if I did? You may be reassured to know that, yes, I definitely have disasters. My first reaction – and advice to you – is to laugh – it is much better than crying.

Once recovered from the shock of the situation, it is time to assess the damage. You have three basic choices: abort, correct or bluff.

ABORT

Before making the decision to give up completely you must be quite certain your dish is truly inedible and cannot possibly be rescued. This being the case you can be:

Honest 'I have been cooking all day and am fed up with it, let's go out to dinner.' Your guests will be much too polite to ask what you have been cooking all day.

Slightly less honest 'I haven't got a vital ingredient and must nip out.' A quick dash to the local take-away follows.

Dishonest 'Has Roger/Sarah told you about his/her diet? We all have to eat salad and Ryvita in this household or he/she feels left out.'

CORRECT

The scope of correcting culinary mishaps is really as broad as cooking itself and needs an entire book devoted to it – my next project? Every disaster requires its own remedy and my best advice is to think laterally and don't worry about what the dish was meant to be – create something new. Here are a few examples:

Lumpy sauces Whisk like mad, then sieve the sauce into a new saucepan.

Burnt flavour Add curry powder, Madeira or black treacle.

No flavour Add a stock cube, sugar or lemon, more salt and pepper and taste again.

Over-seasoned Immediately tip the body of the dish into a sieve, pick out the main ingredients from the sieve to leave the excessive garlic or pepper behind and make an instant new sauce with water, wine and beurre manié.

Boiled dry If the food has not blackened, add water immediately, then re-assess.

Raw meat Carve into thick slices. Heat some butter in a frying pan. Flash fry the meat and flame with brandy. Pour the juices over the meat.

Raw potatoes Slice thinly, then reboil or fry.

Curdled mayonnaise Beat a new yolk in a new dish and very slowly add the curdled mixture.

Scrambled custards Pour immediately through a metal sieve into a glass bowl to cool the mixture.

BLUFF

– THE FINAL SOLUTION

Your end result is nothing like it is meant to be and totally unlike the photograph – but who else knows this?

Parade the dish proudly into the dining-room and announce triumphantly, 'This is something new and I think it will be rather special.' Your guests are bound to agree with you.

INDEX